Computer Programming in JAVA

Computer Programming in JAVA

By

SUDHIR DAWRA

ANMOL PUBLICATIONS PVT. LTD.

NEW DELHI - 110 002 (INDIA)

ANMOL PUBLICATIONS PVT. LTD.
4374/4B, Ansari Road, Daryaganj
New Delhi - 110 002
Ph.: 23261597, 23278000
Visit us at: www.anmolpublications.com

Computer Programming in JAVA

First Published, 2004

PRINTED IN INDIA

Published by J.L. Kumar for Anmol Publications Pvt. Ltd., New Delhi - 110 002 and Printed at Mehra Offset Press, Delhi.

Preface

The present volume is a comprehensive work of information for the students, teachers, programmers. This book primarily deals with programming techniques in JAVA language. JAVA is a language in IT Industry giving solution of all real world problems.

This book is prepared keeping in mind the needs of JAVA programmers. Various methods, functions, servelets, API, Remote Calling and Networking are explained through programming techniques. The book throws light from basic programming to higher Networking level programming.

The book is primarily prepared for students pursuing BCA, B.Tech., MCA & M.Tech. I shall be failing in my duty if I don't acknowledge the contribution of my father Sh. J. K. Dawra and my family members. Last but not the least, I am grateful to Anmol Publications Pvt. Ltd. for undertaking publication of this book.

Any suggestions for improvement of the book would be welcome and gratefully acknowledged and made use in a subsequent edition.

—Sudhir Dawra

Fundamentals, Concepts of JAVA

What is Java?

Java is an object-oriented programming language developed by Sun Microsystems, a company best known for its high-end Unix workstations. Modeled after C++, the Java language was designed to be small, simple, and portable across platforms and operating systems, both at the source and at the binary level.

Java's Past, Present, and Future

The Java language was developed at Sun Microsystems in 1991 as part of a research project to develop software for consumer electronics devices—television sets, VCRs, toasters, and the other sorts of machines you can buy at any department store. Java's goals at that time were to be small, fast, efficient, and easily portable to a wide range of hardware devices. It is those same goals that made Java an ideal language for distributing executable programs via the World Wide Web, and also a general-purpose programming language for developing programs that are easily usable and portable across different platforms.

Sun's 1.0 JDK does include an application called appletviewer that allows you to test your Java applets as you write them. If an applet works in the appletviewer, it should work with any Java-capable browser. You'll learn more about applet viewer later today.

What's in store for the future? In addition to the next Java release from Sun, other companies have announced support for Java in their own World Wide Web browsers. Netscape Communications Corporation has already incorporated Java capabilities into the 2.0 version of their very popular Netscape Navigator Web browser—pages with embedded Java applets can be viewed and played with Netscape. With support for Java available in as popular a browser as Netscape, tools to help develop Java applications (debuggers, development environments, and so on) most likely will be rapidly available as well.

Why Learn Java?

At the moment, probably the most compelling reason to learn Java applets are written in Java. Even if that were not the case, Java as a language has significant advantages over other languages and other programming environments that make it suitable for just about any programming task. This section describes some of those advantages.

Java is Platform-Independent

Platform independence is one of the most significant advantages that Java has over other programming languages, particularly for systems that need to work on many different platforms. Java is platform-independent at both the source and the binary level.

Platform-independence is a program's capability of moving easily from one computer system to another.

At the source level, Java's primitive data types have consistent sizes across all development platforms. Java's foundation class libraries make it easy to write code that can be moved from platform to platform without the need to rewrite it to work with that platform.

Platform-independence doesn't stop at the source level, however. Java binary files are also platform-independent and can run on multiple platforms without the need to recompile the source. How does this work? Java binary files are actually in a form called bytecodes.

Bytecodes are a set of instructions that look a lot like machine code, but are not specific to any one processor.

Normally, when you compile a program written in C or in most other languages, the compiler translates your program into machine codes or processor instructions. Those instructions are specific to the processor your computer is running—so, for example, if you compile your code on a Pentium system, the resulting program will run only on other Pentium systems. If you want to use the same program on another system, you have to go back to your original source, get a compiler for that system, and recompile your code.

Things are different when you write code in Java. The Java development environment has two parts: a Java compiler and a Java interpreter. The Java compiler takes your Java program and instead of generating machine codes from your source files, it generates bytecodes.

To run a Java program, you run a program called a bytecode interpreter, which in turn executes your Java program. You can either run the interpreter by itself, or—for applets—there is a bytecode interpreter built into HotJava and other Java-capable browsers that runs the applet for you.

Why go through all the trouble of adding this extra layer of the bytecode interpreter? Having your Java programs in bytecode form means that instead of being specific to any one system, your programs can be run on any platform and any operating or window system as long as the Java interpreter is available. This capability of a single binary file to be executable across platforms is crucial to what enables applets to work, because the World Wide Web itself is also platform-independent. Just as HTML files can be read on any platform, so applets can be executed on any platform that is a Java-capable browser.

The disadvantage of using bytecodes is in execution speed. Because system-specific programs run directly on the hardware for which they are compiled, they run significantly faster than Java bytecodes, which must be processed by the interpreter. For many Java programs, the speed may not be an issue. If you write programs that require more execution speed than the Java interpreter can provide, you have several solutions available to you, including being able to link native code into your Java program or using tools to convert your Java bytecodes into native code. Note that by using any of these solutions, you lose the portability that Java bytecodes provide.

Java is Object-Oriented

To some, object-oriented programming (OOP) technique is merely a way of organizing programs, and it can be accomplished using any language. Working with a real object-oriented language and programming environment, however, enables you to take full advantage of object-oriented methodology and its capabilities for creating flexible, modular programs and reusing code.

Many of Java's object-oriented concepts are inherited from C++, the language on which it is based, but it borrows many concepts from other object-oriented languages as well. Like most object-oriented programming languages, Java includes a set of class libraries that provide basic data types, system input and output capabilities, and other utility functions. These basic classes are part of the Java development kit, which also has classes to support networking, common Internet protocols, and user interface toolkit functions. Because these class libraries are written in Java, they are portable across platforms as all Java applications are.

Java is Easy to Learn

In addition to its portability and object-orientation, one of Java's initial design goals was to be small and simple, and therefore easier to write, easier to compile, easier to debug, and, best of all, easy to learn. Keeping the language small also makes it more robust because there are fewer chances for programmers to make difficult-to-find mistakes. Despite its size and simple design, however, Java still has a great deal of power and flexibility.

Java is modeled after C and C++, and much of the syntax and object-oriented structure is borrowed from the latter. If you are familiar with C++, learning Java will be particularly easy for you, because you have most of the foundation already.

Although Java looks similar to C and C++, most of the more complex parts of those languages have been excluded from Java, making the language simpler without sacrificing much of its power. There are no pointers in Java, nor is there pointer arithmetic. Strings and arrays are real objects in Java. Memory management is automatic.

To an experienced programmer, these omissions may be difficult to get used to, but to beginners or programmers who have worked in other languages, they make the Java language far easier to learn.

Object Oriented Programming Paradigm and Java

The major motivating factor in the invention of object oriented approach is to salvage some of the flaws encountered in the procedural approach. OOP treats data as a critical element in the program development and does not allow it to flow freely around the system. It ties data more closely to the functions that operate on it and protects it from accidental modification from outside functions. OOP allows us to decompose a problem into a number of entities called objects and then builds data and functions around these entities. The organization of data and functions in object oriented programs is shown in Fig 1. The data of the objects can be accessed only by the functions associated with that object. However, functions of one object can access functions of another object.

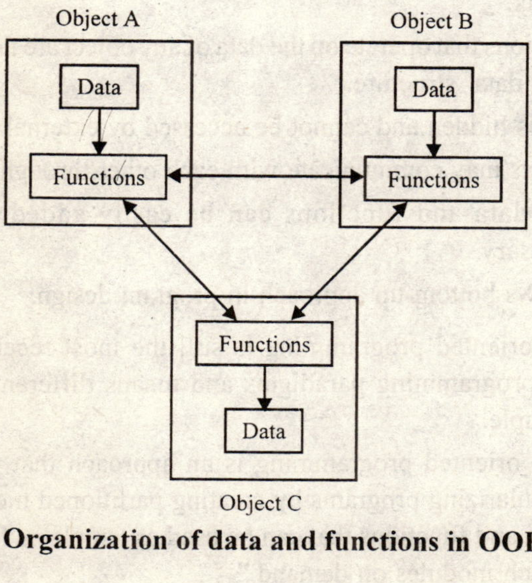

Organization of data and functions in OOP

Object-oriented programming is at the core of Java. In fact, all Java programs are object-oriented. It is 100% object oriented language. Object oriented concepts form the heart of Java just as they form the basis for human understanding. It is important that you understand how these concepts translate into programs. Object-oriented programming is a powerful and natural paradigm for creating programs that survive the inevitable changes accompanying the life cycle of any major software project, including conception, growth, and aging. For example once you have well defined objects and clean, reliable interfaces to those objects, you can gracefully decommission or replace parts of an older system without fear.

OOP is so integral to Java that we must understand its basic principles and its features.

Features of Object Oriented Programming

1. Emphasis on data rather than procedure.
2. Programs are divided into what are known as objects.
3. Data structures are designed such that they characterize the objects.
4. Functions that operate on the data of any object are tied together in the data structure.
5. Data is hidden and cannot be accessed by external functions.
6. Objects may communicate with each other through functions.
7. New data and functions can be easily added whenever necessary.
8. Follows bottom-up approach in program design.

Object oriented programming is still the most recent concept among the programming paradigms and means different things to different people.

"Object oriented programming is an approach that provides a way of modularizing programs by creating partitioned memory area for both data and functions that can be used as templates for creating copies of such modules on demand."

Pillars of OOP

1. Inheritance
2. Encapsulation
3. Abstraction
4. Polymorphism

Inheritance

Inheritance is the process by which objects of one class acquire the properties of the objects of another class. This is important b'coz it supports the concept of hierarchical classification. For example a bird robin is a part of the class flying bird which is again a part of a class bird. The principle is that each derived class shares common characteristics with the class from which it is derived.

In OOP, the concept of inheritance provides the idea of reusability. This means we can add additional features to an existing class without modifying it. This is possible by deriving a new class from an existing class. The new class will have the combined features of both the classes. The real appeal of the inheritance is that it allows the programmer to reuse a class that is almost, but not exactly, what he wants, and to tailor the class in such a way that it does not introduce any undesirable side effects into the rest of the classes.

Encapsulation

Encapsulation is the mechanism that binds together code and the data it manipulates, and keeps both safe from outside interference and misuse. Data encapsulation is the most striking feature of a class. Access to the code and the data inside the wrapper is tightly controlled trough a well defined interface. In JAVA the basis of encapsulation is the class. A class defines the structure and the behavior that will be shared by the objects. Objects are referred to as instances of a class. Thus, a class is a logical construct ;an object has physical reality.

Since the purpose of a class is to encapsulate the complexity, there are mechanisms for hiding the complexity of the complexity of the implementation inside the class. Each method in a class is marked private or public. The *public* interface of the class represents that everything will be accessible to the external users. The *private* interface represents that the members can be accessed by the methods of the class only and not the outside world. This insulation of the data from direct access to the program is called *data hiding.*

Abstraction

Abstraction refers to the act of representing essential features without including the background details or explanations. It is an essential element of OOP. A powerful way to manage abstraction is through the use of hierarchical classifications. This allows you to layer the semantics of complex systems, breaking them into manageable pieces.

Hierarchical abstractions of complex systems can also be applied to computer programs. The data from a traditional process oriented program can be transformed by abstraction into its component objects.

Polymorphism

Polymorphism means the ability to take more than one form. It is a feature that allows one interface to be used for a general class of actions. For example, an operation may exhibit different behavior in different instances. The behavior depends on the type of data used in the operation. If we consider a stack then it might take many forms. There may be integer values or floating point values or it may be a character stack. The algorithm that implements the stack is same even though the data stored differs.

More generally, the concept of polymorphism is often expressed by the phrase "one interface, multiple methods." This means that it is possible to design a generic interface to a group of related activities. This helps to reduce complexity by allowing the same interface to be used to specify a *general class of action*. It is the compiler's job to select the *specific action* as it applies to each situation.

Objects and Classes

Object-oriented programming is modeled on how, in the real world, objects are often made up of many kinds of smaller objects. This capability of combining objects, however, is only one very general aspect of object-oriented programming. Object-oriented programming provides several other concepts and features to make creating and using objects easier and more flexible, and the most important of these features is that of classes.

A *class* is a template for multiple objects with similar features. Classes embody all the features of a particular set of objects.

When you write a program in an object-oriented language, you don't define actual objects. You define classes of objects.

For example, you might have a Tree class that describes the features of all trees (has leaves and roots, grows, creates chlorophyll). The Tree class serves as an abstract model for the concept of a tree—to reach out and grab, or interact with, or cut down a tree you have to have a concrete instance of that tree. Of course, once you have a tree class, you can create lots of different instances of that tree, and each different tree instance can have different features (short, tall, bushy, drops leaves in Autumn), while still behaving like and being immediately recognizable as a tree

An *instance* of a class is another word for an actual object. If class is the general (generic) representation of an object, an instance is its concrete representation.

So what, precisely, is the difference between an instance and an object? Nothing, really. Object is the more general term, but both instances and objects are the concrete representation of a class. In fact, the terms instance and object are often used interchangeably in OOP language. An instance of a tree and a tree object are both the same thing.

In an example closer to the sort of things you might want to do in Java programming, you might create a class for the user interface element called a button. The Button class defines the features of a button (its label, its size, its appearance) and how it behaves (does it need a single click or a double click to activate it, does it change color when it's clicked, what does it do when it's activated?). Once you define the Button class, you can then easily create instances of that button—that is, button objects—that all take on the basic features of the button as defined by the class, but may have different appearances and behavior based on what you want that particular button to do. By creating a Button class, you don't have to keep rewriting the code for each individual button you want to use in your program, and you can reuse the Button class to create different kinds of buttons as you need them in this program and in other programs.

When you write a Java program, you design and construct a set of classes. Then, when your program runs, instances of those classes are created and discarded as needed. Your task, as a Java programmer, is to create the right set of classes to accomplish what your program needs to accomplish.

Fortunately, you don't have to start from the very beginning: the Java environment comes with a library of classes that implement a lot of the basic behavior you need—not only for basic programming tasks (classes to provide basic math functions, arrays, strings, and so on), but also for graphics and networking behavior. In many cases, the Java class libraries may be enough so that all you have to do in your Java program is create a single class that uses the standard class libraries. For complicated Java programs, you may have to create a whole set of classes with defined interactions between them.

A *class library* is a set of classes.

Behavior and Attributes

Every class you write in Java is generally made up of two components: attributes and behavior. In this section, you'll learn about each one as it applies to a thoeretical class called Motorcycle. To finish up this section, you'll create the Java code to implement a representation of a motorcycle.

Attributes

Attributes are the individual things that differentiate one object from another and determine the appearance, state, or other qualities of that object. Let's create a theoretical class called Motorcycle. The attributes of a motorcycle might include the following:

- *Color:* red, green, silver, brown
- *Style:* cruiser, sport bike, standard
- *Make:* Honda, BMW, Bultaco

Attributes of an object can also include information about its state; for example, you could have features for engine condition (off or on) or current gear selected.

Attributes are defined by variables; in fact, you can consider them analogous to "global" variables for the entire object. Because each instance of a class can have different values for its variables, each variable is called an instance variable.

Instance variables define the attributes of an object. The class defines the type of the attribute, and each instance stores its own value for that attribute.

Each attribute, as the term is used here, has a single corresponding instance variable; changing the value of a variable changes the attribute of that object. Instance variables may be set when an object is created and stay constant throughout the life of the object, or they may be able to change at will as the program runs.

In addition to instance variables, there are also class variables, which apply to the class itself and to all its instances. Unlike instance variables, whose values are stored in the instance, class variables' values are stored in the class itself. You'll learn about class variables later on this week; you'll learn more specifics about instance variables tomorrow.

Behavior

A class's behavior determines what instances of that class do to change their internal state changes or when that instance is asked to do something by another class or object. Behavior is the only way objects can do anything to themselves or have anything done to them. For example, to go back to the theoretical Motorcycle class, here are some behaviors that the Motorcycle class might have:

- Start the engine
- Stop the engine
- Speed up
- Change gear
- Stall

To define an object's behavior, you create methods, which look and behave just like functions in other languages, but are defined inside a class. Java does not have functions defined outside classes (as C++ does).

Java Applets and Applications

Java can be used to create two types of programs: applications and applets. An application is a program that runs on your computer, under the operating system of the computer. An applet is an application designed to be transmitted over the internet and executed by a java compatible web browsers. An applet is actually a tiny java program, dynamically downloaded across the networks. The important difference is that an applet is an intelligent program, not just an animation or media file. It can react to user input and dynamically change.

Security

As you are likely aware, every time that you download a "normal" program, you are risking a viral infection. In addition to viruses there are another programs that must be guarded against. This type of program can gather private information such as credit card numbers and passwords. Java answers both these concerns by providing the "Firewall" between a networked application and your computer.

When you use a Java compatible web browser, you can safely download Java applets without fear of viral infection or malicious intent as Java applets are 100% secured programs. Java achieves this protection by confining a Java program to the Java execution environment and not allowing it access to other parts of the computer.

Portability

Many types of computers and operating systems are in the use throughout the world and many are connected to the internet. For programs to be dynamically loaded to all the various types of platforms connected to the internet, some means of generating portable executable code is needed.

Java's Magic: The Bytecode

The key that allows Java to solve both the security and the portability problems is that the output of a Java compiler is not executable code. Rather, it is the bytecode. **Bytecode** is a highly optimized set of instructions designed to be executed by the Java run time system, which is called the **Java Virtual Machine (JVM)**. That is, in its standard form **JVM** is an interpreter for bytecode.

Translating a Java program into bytecode helps makes it much easier to run a program in wide variety of environments. The reason is straightforward: only the **JVM** needs to be implemented for each platform. Once the run time package exists for a given system, any Java program can run on it. Remember, although the details of **JVM** differ from platform to platform, all interpret the same bytecode. Thus, the interpretation of bytecode is the easiest way to cerate truly portable programs.

The fact that a Java program is interpreted also helps in making the program secure. Because the execution of every Java program is under the control of **JVM**, the **JVM** can contain the program and prevent it from generating side effects outside the system.

When a program is interpreted, it generally runs substantially slower than it would run if compiled to executable code. Although Java was designed for interpretation, there is technically nothing about java that prevents on-the-fly compilation of bytecode into native code. Along these lines, Sun has completed its Just In Time (JIT) compiler for bytecode, which is included in the Java 2 release. When the JIT compiler is part of the **JVM**, it compiles bytecode into executable code in real time, on a piece by piece, demand basis. It is not possible to compile an entire Java program into executable code all at once, because Java performs various run time checks that can be only at the run time. Instead the JIT compiles the code as it is needed, during execution.

Features of Java

1. Java is a simple language that can be learned easily.
2. A Java programmer need not know the internals of Java. Unlike C++, Java handles the memory manipulation and thus prevents errors that arise due to improper memory usage.

3. Java is tuned to the web. Java programs can access data across the web easily as they access data from a local system. We can build distributed applications in Java that use resources from any other networked computer.
4. Java is both interpreted and compiled. The code is compiled to a bytecode that is binary and platform independent.
5. Java programs are robust, and bug free and do not crash.
6. Java programs are comparable in speed to the programs written in other compiler based languages like C or C++. Java is faster than other interpreted languages like BASIC since it is compiled and interpreted.
7. Multithreading is the ability of an application to perform multiple tasks at the same time. A single program accomplishes many tasks simultaneously. The core of Java is also multithreaded.

JDK Tools

Java Development Toolkit (JDK) is a software package from Sun Microsystems. JDK provides tools for users to integrate and execute applets and applications. The tools are discussed below.

The javac Compiler

You can create Java programs in any of the text editor. In Java, the source file is called the compilation unit. The java compiler requires that the extension if a java source file is .java.The source code is converted to bytecode by the java compiler. The javac compiler converts the java file to a class file which contains the bytecode.

Syntax for compiling Java code using javac:

```
Javac <filename.java>
```

The java Interpreter

The Java interpreter is used to execute compiled Java applications. The bytecode is the result of compilation is interpreted so that it can be executed.

Syntax for executing a Java application using java:

```
Java < filename.class >
```

The appletviewer

Applets are Java programs that are embedded in web pages. You can run applets using a web browser. The ***appletviewer*** lets your applets without the overhead of running a web browser. You can test your applets using the ***appletviewer.***

Syntax for executing a Java applet:

```
Appletviewer <URL of the .html file>
```

The jdb Tool

Debugging is the term used for identifying and fixing bugs (mistakes) in the program. These mistakes could be syntactical, logical, or runtime (error due to an unexpected condition). You can use the java debugging tool jdb to debug your Java program.

Syntax for using jdb:

```
Jdb <filename.class>
```

The javap Disassembler

If you do not have the .java file but have the bytecode, you can retrieve the Java code using a disassembler. The Java disassembler, javap, is used to recover the source code from the bytecode file.

Syntax for using javap:

```
Javap <list of .class files>
```

The file names should be separated by spaces.

The javadoc Tool

The javadoc is the document generator that creates HTML page documentation for the classes that you create. To use javadoc, you have to embed the statements between /** and */. The javadoc tool has been used by Sun Microsystems for creating Java documentation.

Syntax for using javadoc

```
Javadoc <list of .java files>
```

The file names should be separated by spaces.

The javah Tool

The javah tool creates header and stub files that let you extend your Java code with the C language.

Syntax for creating header files:

```
Javah <class filename>
```

Java Keywords

abstract	Boolean	break	byte	case
catch	Char	class	const	continue
default	Do	double	else	extends
final	Float	finally	for	goto
if	Implements	import	instanceof	int
interface	Long	native	new	package
private	Protected	public	return	short
static	Strictfp	super	switch	synchronized
this	Throw	throws	transient	try
void	Volatile	while		

A First Simple Program

```
/* This is a simple Java program.
   Call this example "Example.java" */
```

```
class Example
   {
        // your program begins with a call to
main()
            public static void main(String args[])
               {
                      System.out.println("This is a
simple Java program.");
               }
        }
```

Entering the Program

For most computer languages, the name of the file that holds the source code to a program is arbitrary. However, this is not the case with Java. The first thing you should remember is that the name you give to a source file is very important. For the above example, the name of the file is "Example.java".

In the example above the name of the class is also Example. This is not a coincidence. In Java, all code must reside inside a class. By convention, the name of the class should match the name of the file that holds the program. You should also make sure that the capitalization of the file name matches the class name. the reason is that Java is case-sensitive.

Compiling the Program

To compile the Example program, execute the compiler, javac, specifying the name of the source file on the command line, as shown here:

```
C:\>javac Example.java
```

The **javac** compiler creates a file called Example.class that contains the bytecode version of the program. The output of **javac** is not the code that can be directly executed.

To actually run the program, you must use the java interpreter, called **java**. To do so , pass the class name Example as a command line argument, as shown below:

```
C:\>java Example
```

When the program is run, the following output is generated on the command line.

This is a simple Java program.

A Closer Look at the First Program

The program begins with the following lines:

```
/* This is a simple Java program.
     Call this example "Example.java" */
```

This is a comment. The contents of a comment are ignored by the compiler. Instead a comment describes the operation of the program to anyone who is reading the source code. Comments are explained later.

The next line of code is

```
class Example{
```

This line uses a keyword **class** to decal that a new class is being defined. Example is an identifier that is the name of the class. The entire class definition, including all of its members, will be between the curly braces{ }.

The next line of code is:

```
public static void main(String args[])
```

This line begins the **main()** method. All Java applications begin execution by calling **main().** The public keyword is an access specifier, which allows the programmer to control the visibility of class members. When a member is declared public then it can be used outside the class also. In this case **main()** must be called public, since it must be called by code outside the class when the program is started. The keyword static allows **main()** to be called without having to instantiate a particular instance of the class. This is necessary since **main()** is called by the java interpreter before any objects are made. The keyword void simply tells the compiler that **main()** does not return a value.

Any information that you need to pass to a method is received by the variables specified within the set of parentheses that follow the name of the method. If there are no parameters required for a given method, you still need to include empty parentheses. In **main()**, there is only one parameter. **String** args[] declares a parameter named args, which is an array of instances of the class **String**. Objects of type **String** store character strings. In this case, args receives any command line arguments present when the program is executed.

Note: **main()** is simply a starting place for the interpreter. A complex program will have dozens of classes, only one of which will need to have the **main()** method to get the things started. The name of the source file is same as the name of the class which defines the **main()** method. When you begin creating applets-Java programs that are embedded in web browsers-you won't use **main()** at all, since a web browser uses a different means of starting the execution of applets.

The next line of code is shown below. Notice that it occurs inside **main()**.

```
System.out.println("This is a simple Java
program.");
```

This line outputs the string "This is a simple Java program." followed by a new line on the screen. Output is actually accomplished by the built-in **println()** method. In this case, **println()** displays the string passed to it. The line begins with **System.out. System** is a predefined class that provides access to the system, and out is the output stream that is connected to the console.

Notice that the above statements end with a semicolon. All statements in Java end with a semicolon.

Variables and Data Types

Variables are locations in memory in which values can be stored. They have a name, a type, and a value. Before you can use a variable, you have to declare it. After it is declared, you can then assign values to it.

Java actually has three kinds of variables: instance variables, class variables, and local variables.

Instance variables, are used to define attributes or the state for a particular object. Class variables are similar to instance variables, except their values apply to all that class's instances (and to the class itself) rather than having different values for each object.

Local variables are declared and used inside method definitions, for example, for index counters in loops, as temporary variables, or to hold values that you need only inside the method definition itself. They can also be used inside blocks ({}), which you'll learn about later this week. Once the method (or block) finishes executing, the variable definition and its value cease to exist. Use local variables to store information needed by a single method and instance variables to store information needed by multiple methods in the object.

Although all three kinds of variables are declared in much the same ways, class and instance variables are accessed and assigned in slightly different ways from local variables.

Note: Unlike other languages, Java does not have global variables—that is, variables that are global to all parts of a program. Instance and class variables can be used to communicate global information between and among objects. Remember, Java is an object-oriented language, so you should think in terms of objects and how they interact, rather than in terms of programs.

Declaring Variables

To use any variable in a Java program, you must first declare it. Variable declarations consist of a type and a variable name:

```
int myAge;
String myName;
boolean isTired;
```

Variable definitions can go anywhere in a method definition (that is, anywhere a regular Java statement can go), although they are most commonly declared at the beginning of the definition before they are used:

```
public static void main (String args[]) {
    int count;
    String title;
    boolean isAsleep;
...
}
```

You can string together variable names with the same type:

```
int x, y, z;
String firstName, LastName;
```

You can also give each variable an initial value when you declare it:

```
int myAge, mySize, numShoes = 28;
String myName = "Laura";
boolean isTired = true;
int a = 4, b = 5, c = 6;
```

If there are multiple variables on the same line with only one initializer (as in the first of the previous examples), the initial value applies to only the last variable in a declaration. You can also group individual variables and initializers on the same line using commas, as with the last example, above.

Local variables must be given values before they can be used (your Java program will not compile if you try to use an unassigned local variable). For this reason, it's a good idea always to give local variables initial values. Instance and class variable definitions do not have this restriction (their initial value depends on the type of the variable: null for instances of classes, 0 for numeric variables, '\0' for characters, and false for booleans).

Notes on Variable Names

Variable names in Java can start with a letter, an underscore (_), or a dollar sign ($). They cannot start with a number. After the first character, your variable names can include any letter or number. Symbols, such as %, *, @, and so on, are often reserved for operators in Java, so be careful when using symbols in variable names.

Finally, note that the Java language is case-sensitive, which means that uppercase letters are different from lowercase letters. This means that the variable *X* is different from the variable x, and a rose is not a Rose is not a ROSE. Keep this in mind as you write your own Java programs and as you read Java code other people have written.

By convention, Java variables have meaningful names, often made up of several words combined. The first word is lowercase, but all following words have an initial uppercase letter:

```
Button theButton;
long reallyBigNumber;
boolean currentWeatherStateOfPlanetXShortVersion;
```

Variable Types

In addition to the variable name, each variable declaration must have a type, which defines what values that variable can hold. The variable type can be one of three things:

- One of the eight basic primitive data types
- The name of a class or interface
- An array

Primitive Data Types

The eight primitive data types handle common types for integers, floating-point numbers, characters, and boolean values (true or false). They're called primitive because they're built into the system and are not actual objects, which makes them more efficient to use. Note that these data types are machine-independent, which means that you can rely on their sizes and characteristics to be consistent across your Java programs.

There are four Java integer types, each with a different range of values (as listed in Table 3.1). All are signed, which means they can hold either positive or negative numbers. Which type you choose for your variables depends on the range of values you expect that variable to hold; if a value becomes too big for the variable type, it is silently truncated.

Integer Types

Type	Size	Range
byte	8 bits	—128 to 127
short	16 bits	—32,768 to 32,767
int	32 bits	—2,147,483,648 to 2,147,483,647
long	64 bits	—9223372036854775808 to 9223372036854775807

Floating-point numbers are used for numbers with a decimal part. Java floating-point numbers are compliant with IEEE 754 (an international standard for defining floating-point numbers and arithmetic). There are two floating-point types: float (32 bits, single-precision) and double (64 bits, double-precision).

The char type is used for individual characters. Because Java uses the Unicode character set, the char type has 16 bits of precision, unsigned.

Finally, the boolean type can have one of two values, true or false. Note that unlike in other C-like languages, boolean is not a number, nor can it be treated as one. All tests of boolean variables should test for true or false.

In addition to the eight basic data types, variables in Java can also be declared to hold an instance of a particular class:

```
String LastName;
Font basicFont;
OvalShape myOval;
```

Each of these variables can then hold only instances of the given class. As you create new classes, you can declare variables to hold instances of those classes (and their subclasses) as well.

Note: Java does not have a typedef statement (as in C and C++). To declare new types in Java, you declare a new class; then variables can be declared to be type of that class

Assigning Values to Variables

Once a variable has been declared, you can assign a value to that variable by using the assignment operator =:

```
size = 14;
tooMuchCaffiene = true;
```

Comments

Java has three kinds of comments. /* and */ surround multiline comments, as in C or C++. All text between the two delimiters is ignored:

```
/* I don't know how I wrote this next part; I was
working really late one night and it just sort of
appeared. I suspect the code elves did it for me.
It might be wise not to try and change it.*/
```

These comments cannot be nested; that is, you cannot have a comment inside a comment.

Double-slashes (//) can be used for a single line of comment. All the text up to the end of the line is ignored:

```
int vices = 7; // are there really only 7 vices?
```

The final type of comment begins with /** and ends with */. The contents of these special comments are used by the javadoc system, but are otherwise used indentically to the first type of comment. Javadoc is used to generate API documentation from the code.

Literals

Literals are used to indicate simple values in your Java programs. Literal is a programming language term, which essentially means that what you type is what you get. For example, if you type 4 in a Java program, you automatically get an integer with the value 4. If you type 'a', you get a character with the value a.

Literals may seem intuitive most of the time, but there are some special cases of literals in Java for different kinds of numbers, characters, strings, and boolean values.

Number Literals

There are several integer literals. 4, for example, is a decimal integer literal of type int (although you can assign it to a variable of type byte or short because it's small enough to fit into those types). A decimal integer literal larger than an int is automatically of type long. You also can force a smaller number to a long by appending an L or l to that number (for example, 4L is a long integer of value 4). Negative integers are preceded by a minus sign—for example, -45.

Integers can also be expressed as octal or hexadecimal: a leading 0 indicates that a number is octal—for example, 0777 or 0004. A leading 0x (or 0X) means that it is in hex (0xFF, 0XAF45). Hexadecimal numbers can contain regular digits (0—9) or upper- or lowercase hex digits (a—f or A—F).

Floating-point literals usually have two parts: the integer part and the decimal part—for example, 5.677777. Floating-point literals result in a floating-point number of type double, regardless of the precision of that number. You can force the number to the type float by appending the letter f (or F) to that number—for example, 2.56F.

You can use exponents in floating-point literals using the letter e or E followed by the exponent (which can be a negative number): 10e45 or .36E-2.

Boolean Literals

Boolean literals consist of the keywords true and false. These keywords can be used anywhere you need a test or as the only possible values for boolean variables.

Character Literals

Character literals are expressed by a single character surrounded by single quotes: 'a', '#', '3', and so on. Characters are stored as 16-bit Unicode characters. The table below lists the special codes that can represent nonprintable characters, as well as characters from the Unicode character set. The letter d in the octal, hex, and Unicode escapes represents a number or a hexadecimal digit (a—f or A—F).

Character Escape Codes

Escape	Meaning
\n	Newline
\t	Tab
\b	Backspace
\r	Carriage return
\f	Formfeed
\\	Backslash
\'	Single quote
\"	Double quote
\ddd	Octal
\xdd	Hexadecimal
\udddd	Unicode character

Note: C and C++ programmers should note that Java does not include character codes for \a (bell) or \v (vertical tab).

String Literals

A combination of characters is a string. Strings in Java are instances of the class String. Strings are not simple arrays of characters as they are in C or C++, although they do have many array-like characteristics (for example, you can test their length and access and change individual characters). Because string objects are real objects in Java, they have methods that enable you to combine, test, and modify strings very easily.

String literals consist of a series of characters inside double quotes:

```
"Hi, I'm a string literal."
"" //an empty string
```

Strings can contain character constants such as newline, tab, and Unicode characters:

```
"A string with a \t tab in it"
"Nested strings are \"strings inside of\" other
strings"
"This string brought to you by Java\u2122"
```

In the last example, the Unicode code sequence for \u2122 produces a trademark symbol (_).

When you use a string literal in your Java program, Java automatically creates an instance of the class String for you with the value you give it. Strings are unusual in this respect; the other literals do not behave in this way (none of the primitive base types are actual objects), and usually creating a new object involves explicitly creating a new instance of a class. You'll learn more about strings, the String class, and the things you can do with strings later today and tomorrow.

Expressions and Operators

Expressions are the simplest form of statement in Java that actually accomplishes something. Expressions are statements that return a value.

Operators are special symbols that are commonly used in expressions.

Arithmetic and tests for equality and magnitude are common examples of expressions. Because they return a value, you can assign that result to a variable or test that value in other Java statements.

Operators in Java include arithmetic, various forms of assignment, increment and decrement, and logical operations. This section describes all these things.

Arithmetic

Java has five operators for basic arithmetic (see Table).

Arithmetic Operators

Operator	Meaning	Example
+	Addition	3+4
—	Subtraction	5—7

Operator	Meaning	Example
*	Multiplication	5 * 5
/	Division	14 / 7
%	Modulus	20 % 7

Each operator takes two operands, one on either side of the operator. The subtraction operator (—) can also be used to negate a single operand.

Integer division results in an integer. Because integers don't have decimal fractions, any remainder is ignored. The expression 31 / 9, for example, results in 3 (9 goes into 31 only 3 times).

Modulus (%) gives the remainder once the operands have been evenly divided. For example, 31 % 9 results in 4 because 9 goes into 31 three times, with 4 left over.

Note that, for integers, the result type of most operations is an int regardless of the original type of the operands. If either or both operands is of type long, the result is of type long. If one operand is an integer and another is a floating point number, the result is a floating point. Listing below is an example of simple arithmetic.

// Simple arithmetic.

```
class ArithmeticTest {
   public static void main (String args[]) {
    short x = 6;
    int y = 4;
    float a = 12.5f;
    float b = 7f;


   System.out.println("x is" + x +", y is" + y);
   System.out.println("x + y = " + (x + y));
   System.out.println("x - y = " + (x - y));
   System.out.println("x / y = " + (x / y));
   System.out.println("x % y = " + (x % y));

   System.out.println("a is" + a +", b is" + b;
   System.out.println("a / b = " + (a / b));
 }
}
```

Output Generated

```
x is 6, y is 4
x + y = 10
x - y = 2
x / y = 1
x % y = 2
a is 12.5, b is 7
a / b = 1.78571
```

In this simple Java application (note the **main()** method), you initially define four variables in lines 3 through 6: x and y, which are integers (type int), and a and b, which are floating-point numbers (type float). Keep in mind that the default type for floating-point literals (such as 12.5) is double, so to make sure these are numbers of type float, you have to use an f after each one (lines 5 and 6).

The remainder of the program merely does some math with integers and floating point numbers and prints out the results.

There is one other thing to mention about this program: the method **System.out.println()**.The **System.out.println()** method merely prints a message to the standard output of your system—to the screen, to a special window, or maybe just to a special log file, depending on your system and the development environment you're running (Sun's JDK prints it to the screen). The **System.out.println()** method takes a single argument—a string—but you can use + to concatenate values into a string, as you'll learn later today.

More About Assignment

Variable assignment is a form of expression; in fact, because one assignment expression results in a value, you can string them together like this:

```
x = y = z = 0;
```

In this example, all three variables now have the value 0.

The right side of an assignment expression is always evaluated before the assignment takes place. This means that expressions such as x = x + 2 do the right thing; 2 is added to the value of x, and then that new value is reassigned to x. In fact, this sort of operation is so common that Java has several operators to do a shorthand version of this, borrowed from C and C++. Table shows these shorthand assignment operators.

Assignment Operators

Expression	Meaning
x+=y	x=x+y
x−=y	x=x−y
x*=y	x=x*y
x/=y	x=x/y

Incrementing and Decrementing

As in C and C++, the ++ and — operators are used to increment or decrement a value by 1. For example, x++ increments the value of x by 1 just as if you had used the expression x = x + 1. Similarly x — decrements the value of x by 1. (Unlike C and C++, Java allows x to be floating point.)

These increment and decrement operators can be prefixed or postfixed; that is, the ++ or — can appear before or after the value it increments or decrements. For simple increment or decrement expressions, which one you use isn't overly important. In complex assignments, where you are assigning the result of an increment or decrement expression, which one you use makes a difference.

Take, for example, the following two expressions:

```
y = x++;
y = ++x;
```

These two expressions give very different results because of the difference between prefix and postfix. When you use postfix operators (x++ or x—), y gets the value of x before x is changed; using prefix, the value of x is assigned to y after the change has occurred. Listing below is a Java example of how all this works.

// Test of prefix and postfix increment operators.

```
class PrePostFixTest {
   public static void main (String args[]) {
      int x = 0;
      int y = 0;
      System.out.println("x and y are " + x + " and
" + y );
      x++;
      System.out.println("x++ results in " + x);
      ++x;
      System.out.println("++x results in " + x);
      System.out.println("Resetting x back to 0.");
      x = 0;
      System.out.println("———————");
      y = x++;
      System.out.println("y = x++ (postfix) results
in:");
      System.out.println("x is " + x);
      System.out.println("y is " + y);
      System.out.println("———————");
      y = ++x;
      System.out.println("y = ++x (prefix) results
in:");
      System.out.println("x is " + x);
      System.out.println("y is " + y);
   }
}
```

Output Generated

```
x and y are 0 and 0
x++ results in 1
++x results in 2
Resetting x back to 0.
———————
y = x++ (postfix) results in:
x is 1
y is 0
———————
y = ++x (prefix) results in:
x is 2
y is 2
```

In the first part of this example, you increment x alone using both prefix and postfix increment operators. In each, x is incremented by 1 each time. In this simple form, using either prefix or postfix works the same way.

In the second part of this example, you use the expression y = x++, in which the postfix increment operator is used. In this result, the value of x is incremented *after* that value is assigned to y. Hence the result: y is assigned the original value of x (0), and then x is incremented by 1.

In the third part, you use the prefix expression y = ++x. Here, the reverse occurs: x is incremented before its value is assigned to y. Because x is 1 from the previous step, its value is incremented (to 2), and then that value is assigned to y. Both x and y end up being 2.

Note: Technically, this description is not entirely correct. In reality, Java *always* completely evaluates all expressions on the right of an expression before assigning that value to a variable, so the concept of "assigning x to y before x is incremented" isn't precisely right. Instead, Java takes the value of x and "remembers" it, evaluates (increments) x, and *then* assigns the original value of x to y. Although in most simple cases this distinction may not be important, for more complex expressions with side effects it may change the behavior of the expression overall..

Comparisons

Java has several expressions for testing equality and magnitude. All of these expressions return a boolean value (that is, true or false). Table 3.5 shows the comparison operators:

Comparison Operators

Operator	Meaning	Example
==	Equal	x=3
!=	Not equal	x!=3
<	Less than	x<3

Operator	Meaning	Example
>	Greater than	x>3
<=	Less than or equal to	x<=3
>=	Greater than or equal to	x>=3

Logical Operators

Expressions that result in boolean values (for example, the comparison operators) can be combined by using logical operators that represent the logical combinations AND, OR, XOR, and logical NOT.

For AND combinations, use either the & or &&. The expression will be true only if both expressions are also true; if either expression is false, the entire expression is false. The difference between the two operators is in expression evaluation. Using &, both sides of the expression are evaluated regardless of the outcome. Using &&, if the left side of the expression is false, the entire expression returns false, and the right side of the expression is never evaluated.

For OR expressions, use either | or ||. OR expressions result in true if either or both of the operands is also true; if both operands are false, the expression is false. As with & and &&, the single | evaluates both sides of the expression regardless of the outcome; with ||, if the left expression is true, the expression returns true and the right side is never evaluated.

In addition, there is the XOR operator ^, which returns true only if its operands are different (one true and one false, or vice versa) and false otherwise (even if both are true).

In general, only the && and || are commonly used as actual logical combinations. &, |, and ^ are more commonly used for bitwise logical operations.

For NOT, use the ! operator with a single expression argument. The value of the NOT expression is the negation of the expression; if x is true, !x is false.

Operator Precedence

<table>
<tr><th>Operator</th><th>Notes</th></tr>
<tr><td>. [] ()</td><td>Parentheses () group expressions; dot (.) is used for access to methods and variables within objects and classes (discussed tomorrow); [] is used for arrays (discussed later on in the week)</td></tr>
<tr><td>++ —— ! ~</td><td>Returns true or false based on whether the object</td></tr>
<tr><td>instanceof</td><td>is an instance of the named class or any of that class's superclasses (discussed tomorrow)</td></tr>
<tr><td>new (type) expression</td><td>The new operator is used for creating new instances of classes; () in this case is for casting a value to another type (you'll learn about both of these tomorrow)</td></tr>
<tr><td>* / %</td><td>Multiplication, division, modulus</td></tr>
<tr><td>+ —</td><td>Addition, subtraction</td></tr>
<tr><td><< >> >>></td><td>Bitwise left and right shift</td></tr>
<tr><td>< > <= >=</td><td>Relational comparison tests</td></tr>
<tr><td>== !=</td><td>Equality</td></tr>
<tr><td>&</td><td>AND</td></tr>
<tr><td>^</td><td>XOR</td></tr>
<tr><td>|</td><td>OR</td></tr>
<tr><td>&&</td><td>Logical AND</td></tr>
<tr><td>||</td><td>Logical OR</td></tr>
<tr><td>? :</td><td>Shorthand for if...then...else (discussed on Day 5)</td></tr>
<tr><td>= += —= *= /=
%= ^= &= |= <<
=>>= >>>=</td><td>Various assignments</td></tr>
</table>

Operator precedence determines the order in which expressions are evaluated. This, in some cases, can determine the overall value of the expression. For example, take the following expression:

```
y = 6 + 4 / 2
```

Depending on whether the 6 + 4 expression or the 4 / 2 expression is evaluated first, the value of y can end up being 5 or 8. Operator precedence determines the order in which expressions are evaluated, so you can predict the outcome of an expression. In general, increment and decrement are evaluated before arithmetic, arithmetic expressions are evaluated before comparisons, and comparisons are evaluated before logical expressions. Assignment expressions are evaluated last.

The table below shows the specific precedence of the various operators in Java. Operators further up in the table are evaluated first; operators on the same line have the same precedence and are evaluated left to right based on how they appear in the expression itself. For example, give that same expression y = 6 + 4 / 2, you now know, according to this table, that division is evaluated before addition, so the value of y will be 8.

Operator Precedence

You can always change the order in which expressions are evaluated by using parentheses around the expressions you want to evaluate first. You can nest parentheses to make sure expressions evaluate in the order you want them to (the innermost parenthetical expression is evaluated first). The following expression results in a value of 5, because the 6 + 4 expression is evaluated first, and then the result of that expression (10) is divided by 2:

```
y = (6 + 4) / 2
```

Parentheses also can be useful in cases where the precedence of an expression isn't immediately clear—in other words, they can make your code easier to read.

String Arithmetic

One special expression in Java is the use of the addition operator (+) to create and concatenate strings. In most of the previous examples shown today and in earlier lessons, you've seen lots of lines that looked something like this:

```
System.out.println(name + " is a " + color "
beetle");
```

The output of that line (to the standard output) is a single string, with the values of the variables (here, name and color), inserted in the appropriate spots in the string. So what's going on here?

The + operator, when used with strings and other objects, creates a single string that contains the concatenation of all its operands. If any of the operands in string concatenation is not a string, it is automatically converted to a string, making it easy to create these sorts of output lines.

Note: An object or type can be converted to a string if you implement the method toString(). All objects have a default string representation, but most classes override toString() to provide a more meaningful printable representation.

String concatenation makes lines such as the previous one especially easy to construct. To create a string, just add all the parts together—the descriptions plus the variables—and output it to the standard output, to the screen, to an applet, or anywhere.

The += operator, which you learned about earlier, also works for strings. For example, take the following expression:

```
myName += " Jr.";
```

This expression is equivalent to this:

```
myName = myName + " Jr.";
```

just as it would be for numbers. In this case, it changes the value of myName (which might be something like John Smith to have a Jr. at the end (John Smith Jr.).

Arrays

Arrays in Java are different than they are in other languages. Arrays in Java are actual objects that can be passed around and treated just like other objects.

Arrays are a way to store a list of items. Each slot of the array holds an individual element, and you can place elements into or change the contents or those slots as you need to.

Arrays can contain any type of element value (primitive types or objects), but you can't store different types in a single array. You can have an array of integers, or an array of strings, or an array of arrays, but you can't have an array that contains, for example, both strings and integers.

To create an array in Java, you use three steps:

1. Declare a variable to hold the array.
2. Create a new array object and assign it to the array variable.
3. Store things in that array.

Declaring Array Variables

The first step to creating an array is creating a variable that will hold the array, just as you would any other variable. Array variables indicate the type of object the array will hold (just as they do for any variable) and the name of the array, followed by empty brackets ([]). The following are all typical array variable declarations:

```
String difficultWords[];
Point hits[];
int temps[];
```

An alternate method of defining an array variable is to put the brackets after the type instead of after the variable. They are equivalent, but this latter form is often much more readable. So, for example, these three declarations could be written like this:

```
String[] difficultWords;
Point[] hits;
int[] temps;
```

Creating Array Objects

The second step is to create an array object and assign it to that variable. There are two ways to do this:

- Using new
- Directly initializing the contents of that array

The first way is to use the new operator to create a new instance of an array:

```
String[] names = new String[10];
```

That line creates a new array of Strings with ten *slots*, containing elements. When you create a new array object using new, you must indicate how many slots that array will hold.

Array objects can contain primitive types such as integers or booleans, just as they can contain objects:

```
int[] temps = new int[99];
```

When you create an array object using new, all its slots are initialized for you (0 for numeric arrays, false for boolean, '\0' for character arrays, and null for objects). You can also create and initialize an array at the same time. Instead of using new to create the new array object, enclose the elements of the array inside braces, separated by commas:

```
String[] chiles = { "jalapeno", "anaheim",
"serrano",
    "habanero", "thai" };
```

Each of the elements inside the braces must be of the same type and must be the same type as the variable that holds that array. An array the size of the number of elements you've included will be automatically created for you. This example creates an array of String objects named chiles that contains five elements.

Multidimensional Arrays

Java does not support multidimensional arrays. However, you can declare and create an array of arrays (and those arrays can contain arrays, and so on, for however many dimensions you need), and access them as you would C-style multidimensional arrays:

```
int coords[][] = new int[12][12];
coords[0][0] = 1;
coords[0][1] = 2;
```

Block Statements

A block statement is a group of other statements surrounded by braces ({}). You can use a block anywhere a single statement would go, and the new block creates a new local scope for the statements inside it. This means that you can declare and use local variables inside a block, and those variables will cease to exist after the block is finished executing. For example, here's a block inside a method definition that declares a new variable y. You cannot use y outside the block in which it's declared:

```
void testblock() {
    int x = 10;
    { // start of block
      int y = 50;
      System.out.println("inside the block:");
      System.out.println("x:" + x);
      System.out.println("y:" + y);
    } // end of block
}
```

Blocks are not usually used in this way—alone in a method definition. You've mostly seen blocks up to this point surrounding class and method definitions, but another very common use of block statements is in the control flow constructs you'll learn about in the remainder of today's lesson.

if Conditionals

The if conditional, which enables you to execute different bits of code based on a simple test in Java, is nearly identical to if statements in C. if conditionals contain the keyword if, followed by a boolean test, followed by a statement (often a block statement) to execute if the test is true:

```
if (x < y)
    System.out.println("x is smaller than y");
```

An optional else keyword provides the statement to execute if the test is false:

```
if (x < y)
    System.out.println("x is smaller than y");
else System.out.println("y is bigger");

if (engineState == true )
    System.out.println("Engine is already on.");
else {
    System.out.println("Now starting Engine.");
     if (gasLevel >= 1)
         engineState = true;
    else System.out.println("Low on gas! Can't
start engine.");
}
```

This example uses the test (engineState == true). For boolean tests of this type, a common shortcut is merely to include the first part of the expression, rather than explicitly testing its value against true or false:

```
if (engineState)
    System.out.println("Engine is on.");
else System.out.println("Engine is off.");
```

The Conditional Operator

An alternative to using the if and else keywords in a conditional statement is to use the conditional operator, sometimes called the ternary operator.

The *conditional operator* is a *ternary operator* because it has three terms.

The conditional operator is an expression, meaning that it returns a value (unlike the more general if, which only can result in a statement or block being executed). The conditional operator is most useful for very short or simple conditionals, and looks like this:

```
test ? trueresult : falseresult
```

The *test* is an expression that returns true or false, just like the test in the if statement. If the test is true, the conditional operator returns the value of *trueresult*; if it's false, it returns the value of *falseresult*. For example, the following conditional tests the values of x and y, returns the smaller of the two, and assigns that value to the variable smaller:

```
int smaller = x < y ? x : y;
```

The conditional operator has a very low precedence; that is, it's usually evaluated only after all its subexpressions are evaluated. The only operators lower in precedence are the assignment operators. See the precedence chart in Day 3's lesson for a refresher on precedence of all the operators.

Switch Conditionals

A common programming practice in any language is to test a variable against some value, and if it doesn't match that value, to test it again against a different value, and if it doesn't match that one to make yet another test, and so on. Using only if statements, this can become unwieldy, depending on how it's formatted and how many different options you have to test. For example, you might end up with a set of if statements something like this or longer:

```
if (oper == '+')
  addargs(arg1, arg2);
else if (oper == '-')
   subargs(arg1, arg2);
else if (oper == '*')
   multargs(arg1, arg2);
else if (oper == '/')
   divargs(arg1, arg2);
```

This form of if statement is called a **nested** if, because each else statement in turn contains yet another if, and so on, until all possible tests have been made.

A common shorthand mechanism for nested ifs that you can use in some cases allows you to group tests and actions together in a single statement. This is the switch or case statement; in Java it's switch and behaves as it does in C:

```
switch (]test) {
    case valueOne:
            resultOne;
      break;
    case valueTwo:
            resultTwo;
      break;
    case valueThree:
            resultThree;
      break;
    ...
    default: defaultresult;
}
```

In the switch statement, the test (a primitive type of byte, char, short, or int) is compared with each of the case values in turn. If a match is found, the statement, or statements after the test is executed. If no match is found, the default statement is executed. The default is optional, so if there isn't a match in any of the cases and default doesn't exist, the switch statement completes without doing anything.

Note that the significant limitation of the switch in Java is that the tests and values can be only simple primitive types (and then only primitive types that are castable to int). You cannot use larger primitive types (long, float), strings, or other objects within a switch, nor can you test for any relationship other than equality. This limits the usefulness of switch to all but the simplest cases; nested ifs can work for any kind of test on any type.

Here's a simple example of a switch statement similar to the nested if shown earlier:

```
switch (oper) {
    case '+':
        addargs(arg1, arg2);
        break;
    case '*':
        subargs(arg1, arg2);
        break;
    case '-':
        multargs(arg1, arg2);
        break;
```

```
      case '/':
          divargs(arg1, arg2);
          break;
  }
```

Note the break statement included in every line. Without the explicit break, once a match is made, the statements for that match and also all the statements further down in the switch are executed until a break or the end of the switch is found (and then execution continues after the end of the switch). In some cases, this may be exactly what you want to do, but in most cases, you'll want to make sure to include the break so that only the statements you want to be executed are executed.

One handy use of falling through occurs when you want multiple values to execute the same statements. In this instance, you can use multiple case lines with no result, and the switch will execute the first statements it finds. For example, in the following switch statement, the string "x is an even number." is printed if x has values of 2, 4, 6, or 8. All other values of x print the string "x is an odd number."

```
switch (x) {
    case 2:
    case 4:
    case 6:
    case 8:
       System.out.println("x is an even number.");
        break;
   default: System.out.println("x is an odd
number.");
}
```

for Loops

The **for** loop, repeats a statement or block of statements some number of times until a condition is matched. for loops are frequently used for simple iteration in which you repeat a block of statements a certain number of times and then stop, but you can use for loops for just about any kind of loop.

Syntax of for loop:

```
for (initialization; test; increment) {
    statements;

}
```

The start of the for loop has three parts:

- initialization is an expression that initializes the start of the loop. If you have a loop index, this expression might declare and initialize it, for example, int i = 0. Variables that you declare in this part of the for loop are local to the loop itself; they cease existing after the loop is finished executing.
- test is the test that occurs after each pass of the loop. The test must be a boolean expression or function that returns a boolean value, for example, i < 10. If the test is true, the loop executes. Once the test is false, the loop stops executing.
- increment is any expression or function call. Commonly, the increment is used to change the value of the loop index to bring the state of the loop closer to returning false and completing.

The statement part of the for loop is the statements that are executed each time the loop iterates. Just as with if, you can include either a single statement here or a block; the previous example used a block because that is more common. Here's an example of a for loop that initializes all the values of a String array to null strings:

```
String strArray[] = new String[10];
int i; // loop index
for (i = 0; i < strArray.length; i++)
    strArray[i] = "";
```

Any of the parts of the for loop can be empty statements, that is, you can simply include a semicolon with no expression or statement, and that part of the for loop will be ignored. Note that if you do use a null statement in your for loop, you may have to initialize or increment any loop variables or loop indices yourself elsewhere in the program.

You can also have an empty statement for the body of your for loop, if everything you want to do is in the first line of that loop. For example, here's one that finds the first prime number higher than 4000:

```
for (i = 4001; notPrime(i); i += 2)
    ;
```

Note: A common mistake in C that also occurs in Java is to accidentally put a semicolon after the first line of the for loop:

```
for (i = 0; i < 10; i++);
System.out.println("Loop!");
```

Because the first semicolon ends the loop with an empty statement, the loop doesn't actually do anything. The println() method will be printed only once, because it's actually outside the for loop entirely.

---

while Loops

The **while** loop is used to repeat a statement or block of statements as long as a particular condition is true.

Syntax of while loop:

```
while (condition) {
    bodyOfLoop;
}
```

The *condition* is a boolean expression. If it returns true, the while loop executes the statements in bodyOfLoop and then tests the condition again, repeating until the condition is false.

Here's an example of a while loop that copies the elements of an array of integers (in array1) to an array of floats (in array2), casting each element to a float as it goes. The one catch is that if any of the elements in the first array is 0, the loop will immediately exit at that point. To cover both the cases wherein all the elements have been copied and an element is 0, you can use a compound test with the && operator:

```
int count = 0;
while ( count < array1.length && array1[count] !=0)
{
    array2[count] = (float) array1[count++];
}
```

Note that if the condition is initially false the first time it is tested (for example, if the first element in that first array is 0), the body of the while loop will never be executed. If you need ιo execute the loop at least once, you can do one of two things:

- Duplicate the body of the loop outside the while loop.
- Use a do loop (described below).

The do loop is considered the better solution of the two.

do...while Loops

The **do loop** is just like a while loop, except that do executes a given statement or block until the condition is false. The main difference is that while loops test the condition before looping, making it possible that the body of the loop will never execute if the condition is false the first time it's tested. do loops run the body of the loop at least once before testing the condition. do loops look like this:

```
do {
    bodyOfLoop;
} while (condition);
```

Here, the bodyOfLoop part is the statements that are executed with each iteration. It's shown here with a block statement because it's most commonly used that way, but you can substitute the braces for a single statement as you can with the other control-flow constructs. The condition is a boolean test. If it returns true, the loop is run again. If it returns false, the loop exits. Keep in mind that with do loops, the body of the loop executes at least once.

Here's a simple example of a do loop that prints a message each time the loop iterates:

```
int x = 1;
do {
    System.out.println("Looping, round " + x);
    x++;
} while (x <= 10);
```

Here's the **output** of these statements:

```
Looping, round 1
Looping, round 2
Looping, round 3
Looping, round 4
Looping, round 5
Looping, round 6
Looping, round 7
Looping, round 8
Looping, round 9
Looping, round 10
```

Breaking Out of Loops

In all the loops (for, while, and do), the loop ends when the condition you're testing for is met. What happens if something odd occurs within the body of the loop and you want to exit the loop early? For that, you can use the break and continue keywords.

You've already seen break as part of the switch statement; it stops execution of the switch, and the program continues. The break keyword, when used with a loop, does the same thing—it immediately halts execution of the current loop. If you've nested loops within loops, execution picks up in the next outer loop; otherwise, the program merely continues executing the next statement after the loop.

For example, take that while loop that copied elements from an integer array into an array of floats until the end of the array or until a 0 is reached. You can test for that latter case inside the body of the while and then use a break to exit the loop:

```
int count = 0;
while (count < array1.length) {
    if (array1[count] == 0) {
        break;
    }
    array2[count] = (float) array1[count++];
}
```

continue is similar to break except that instead of halting execution of the loop entirely, the loop starts over at the next iteration. For do and while loops, this means the execution of the block starts over again; for for loops, the increment expression is evaluated and then the block is executed. continue is useful when you want to special-case elements within a loop. With the previous example of copying one array to another, you can test for whether the current element is 0 and restart the loop if you find it so that the resulting array will never contain zero. Note that because you're skipping elements in the first array, you now have to keep track of two different array counters:

```
int count1 = 0;
int count2 = 0;
while (count < array1.length) {
    if (array1[count] == 0)
        continue;
    array2[count2++] = (float)array1[count++];
}
foo:
    for (int i = 1; i <= 5; i++)
        for (int j = 1; j <= 3; j++) {
            System.out.println("i is " + i + ", j
is " + j);
            if ((i + j) > 4)
                break foo;
        }
System.out.println("end of loops");
```

Here's the output from this program:

```
i is 1, j is 1
i is 1, j is 2
i is 1, j is 3
i is 2, j is 1
i is 2, j is 2
i is 2, j is 3
end of loops
```

As you can see, the loop iterated until the sum of i and j was greater than 4, and then both loops exited back to the outer block and the final message was printed.

return Statement

The last control statement is **return**. The **return** statement is used to explicitly return from a method. That is, it causes program control to transfer back to the caller of the method. It is categorized as a jump statement. At any time in a method the **return** statement can be used to cause execution to branch back to the caller of the method. Thus, the **return** statement immediately terminates the method in which it is executed.

Defining Classes

Defining classes is pretty easy; To define a class, use the class keyword and the name of the class. A class definition with nothing in it is pretty dull; usually, when you create a class, you have something you want to add to make that class different from other classes. Inside each class definition are declarations and definitions for variables or methods or both for the class *and* for each instance.

```
class MyClassName {
type instance-var1;
type instance-var2;
//...
type instance-varN;

type methodname1(parameter-list){
// body of method
}
type methodname1(parameter-list){
// body of method
}
//...
type methodnameN(parameter-list){
// body of method
}

}
```

Defining Instance Variables

Instance variables, fortunately, are declared and defined in almost exactly the same way as local variables; the main difference is their location in the class definition. Variables are considered instance variables if they are declared outside a method definition. Customarily, however, most instance variables are defined just after the first line of the class definition. For example, Listing 6.1 shows a simple class definition for the class Box. This class definition contains three instance variables.

// A program that uses the Box class

```
class Box{
  double width;
  double height;
  double depth;
}

// This class declares an object of type Box
class BoxDemo{
   public static void main(String args[])
        {
                Box mybox=new Box();
                Double vol;
                mybox.width=10;
                mybox.height=20;
                mybox.depth=15;
                vol= mybox.width * mybox.height  *
mybox.depth;
                System.out.println("The volume of the
box is " + vol);
        }
}
```

We call the file BoxDemo.java b'coz it contains the main() method. When we compile this code we seethat two .class files have been created, one for the class Box and other for class BoxDemo. The output of the above program is :

```
The volume of the box is 3000.0
```

Each object has its own copy of the variables. If we would have two objects then both of them would have their own copies of the variables.

Constants

Constants are useful for defining shared values for all the methods of an object—for giving meaningful names to object-wide values that will never change. In Java, you can create constants only for instance or class variables, not for local variables.

A *constant variable* or *constant* is a variable whose value never changes (which may seem strange given the meaning of the word "variable").

To declare a constant, use the **final** keyword before the variable declaration and include an initial value for that variable:

```
final float pi = 3.141592;
final boolean debug = false;
final int maxsize = 40000;
```

Declaring Objects

When you create a class you are creating a new data type. You can use this to declare objects of this type. However, obtaining objects of a class is a two step process. First, you must declare a variable of the class type. This variable does not define an object. Instead, it is simply a variable which can refer to an object. Second, you must acquire an actual, physical copy of the object and assign it to that variable. This is done with the help of **new** operator. The **new** operator dynamically allocates memory for an object and returns the reference to it. This reference is the memory address of the object allocated by **new**. This reference is then stored in the variable. Thus, in Java, all class objects are dynamically allocated. In the example above an object of class Box was declared as follows:

```
Box mybox =new Box();
```

This step combines the two steps described above. It can be rewritten like this to show each step more clearly.

```
Box mybox;  // declare reference to object
Mybox = new Box();  // allocate a Box object
```

The first line declares mybox as a reference to an object of type Box. After this line executes, mybox contains **null,** which indicates that it does not yet point to any actual object. The next line allocates an actual object and assigns a reference to mybox. After the second line you can use mybox as if it were a Box object. But in reality, mybox simply holds the memory address of the actual Box object.

Creating Methods

Methods, define an object's behavior—what happens when that object is created and the various operations that object can perform during its lifetime.

Defining Methods

Method definitions have four basic parts:

- The name of the method
- The type of object or primitive type the method returns
- A list of parameters
- The body of the method

The method's ***signature*** is a combination of the name of the method, the type of object or base type this method returns, and a list of parameters.

In other languages, the name of the method (or function, subroutine, or procedure) is enough to distinguish it from other methods in the program. In Java, you can have different methods that have the same name but a different return type or argument list. This is called method overloading

Here's what a basic method definition looks like:

```
returntype methodname(type1 arg1, type2 arg2, type3
arg3..) {
    ...
}
```

The *returntype* is the primitive type or class of the of the value this method returns. It can be one of the primitive types, a class name, or void if the method does not return a value at all.

Note that if this method returns an array object, the array brackets can go either after the return type or after the parameter list; because the former way is considerably easier to read, it is used in the examples today (and throughout this book):

```
int[] makeRange(int lower, int upper) {...}
```

The method's parameter list is a set of variable declarations, separated by commas, inside parentheses. These parameters become local variables in the body of the method, whose values are the objects or values of primitives passed in when the method is called.

// A program that shows how to use a method inside the Box class

```
class Box{
  double width;
  double height;
  double depth;

// display volume of the box
   void volume(){
     System.out.print("The volume of the box is ");
    System.out.println(width*height*depth);
 }
}

// This class declares an object of type Box
class BoxDemo{
   public static void main(String args[])
         {
               Box mybox=new Box();
               Double vol;
               mybox.width=10;
               mybox.height=20;
               mybox.depth=15;
               mybox.volume();
         }
 }
```

The line of code mybox.volume() invokes the method on mybox. That is, it callas volume relative to mybox object using the dot operator.

The this Keyword

In the body of a method definition, you may want to refer to the current object—the object the method was called on— to refer to that object's instance variables or to pass the current object as an argument to another method. To refer to the current object in these cases, you can use the this keyword. this refers to the current object, and you can use it anywhere that object might appear—in dot notation to refer to the object's instance variables, as an argument to a method, as the return value for the current method, and so on. Here's an example:

```
t = this.x              // the x instance variable for
                           this object
this.myMethod(this)     // call the mymethod method,
                           defined in
                        // this class, and pass it the
                           current
                        // object
return this;            // return the current object
```

In many cases, however, you may be able to omit the this keyword. You can refer to both instance variables and method calls defined in the current class simply by name; the this is implicit in those references. So, the first two examples could be written like this:

```
t = x                   // the x instance variable for
                           this object
myMethod(this)          // call the myMethod method,
                           defined in this
                        // class
```

Keep in mind that because this is a reference to the current instance of a class, therefore you should only use it inside the body of an instance method definition. Class methods, that is, methods declared with the static keyword, cannot use this.

Variable Scope and Method Definitions

When you refer to a variable within your method definitions, Java checks for a definition of that variable first in the current scope (which may be a block), then in the outer scopes up to the current method definition. If that variable is not a local variable, Java then checks for a definition of that variable as an instance or class variable in the current class, and then, finally, in each superclass in turn.

Because of the way Java checks for the scope of a given variable, it is possible for you to create a variable in a lower scope such that a definition of that same variable "hides" the original value of that variable. This can introduce subtle and confusing bugs into your code.

For example, note this small Java program:

```
class ScopeTest {
    int test = 10;
    void printTest () {
        int test = 20;
        System.out.println("test = " + test);
    }
}
```

In this class, you have two variables with the same name and definition: the first, an instance variable, has the name test and is initialized to the value 10. The second is a local variable with the same name, but with the value 20. Because the local variable hides the instance variable, the println() method will print that test is 20.

You can get around this particular problem by using this.test to refer to the instance variable, and just test to refer to the local variable.

A more insidious example of this occurs when you redefine a variable in a subclass that already occurs in a superclass. This can create very subtle bugs in your code—for example, you may call methods that are intended to change the value of an instance variable, but that change the wrong one. Another bug might occur when you cast an object from one class to another—the value of your instance variable may mysteriously change (because it was getting that value from the superclass instead of from your class). The best way to avoid this behavior is to make sure that, when you define variables in a subclass, you're aware of the variables in each of that class's superclasses and you don't duplicate what is already there.

Passing Arguments to Methods

When you call a method with object parameters, the variables you pass into the body of the method are passed by reference, which means that whatever you do to those objects inside the method affects the original objects as well. This includes arrays and all the objects that arrays contain; when you pass an array into a method and modify its contents, the original array is affected. (Note that primitive types are passed by value.)

More About Methods

Methods are arguably the most important part of any object-oriented language. Whereas classes and objects provide the framework, and class and instance variables provide a way of holding that class or object's attributes and state, it is the methods that actually provide an object's behavior and define how that object interacts with other objects in the system.

Some additional features of methods are given below:

- ***Overloading methods***—that is, creating methods with multiple signatures and definitions but with the same name
- ***Creating constructor methods***—methods that enable you to initialize objects to set up their initial state when created
- ***Overriding methods***—creating a different definition for a method that has been defined in a superclass
- ***Finalizer methods***—a way for an object to clean up after itself before it is removed from the system

Creating Methods with the Same Name, Different Arguments

Methods in Java can also be overloaded—that is, you can create methods that have the same name, but different signatures and different definitions. Method overloading enables instances of your class to have a simpler interface to other objects (no need for entirely different methods that do essentially the same thing) and to behave differently based on the input to that method.

When you call a method in an object, Java matches up the method name and the number and type of arguments to choose which method definition to execute.

To create an overloaded method, all you need to do is create several different method definitions in your class, all with the same name, but with different parameter lists (either in number or type of arguments). Java allows method overloading as long as each parameter list is unique for the same method name.

Note that Java differentiates overloaded methods with the same name, based on the number and type of parameters to that method, not on its return type. That is, if you try to create two methods with the same name, same parameter list, but different return types, you'll get a compiler error. The variable names you choose for each parameter to the method are irrelevant—all that matters is the number and the type.

Here's an example of creating an overloaded method. The program below shows a simple class definition for a class called MyRect, which defines a rectangular shape. The MyRect class has four instance variables to define the upper left and lower right corners of the rectangle: x1, y1, x2, and y2.

Note: Why did I call it MyRect? Java's awt package has a class called Rectangle that implements much of this same behavior. I called this class MyRect to prevent confusion between the two classes.

// Demonstration of overloaded methods.

```
import java.awt.Point;
class MyRect {
    int x1 = 0;
    int y1 = 0;
    int x2 = 0;
    int y2 = 0;
```

```
MyRect buildRect(int x1, int y1, int x2, int y2)
    {
        this.x1 = x1;
        this.y1 = y1;
        this.x2 = x2;
        this.y2 = y2;
        return this;
    }
MyRect buildRect(Point topLeft, Point bottomRight)
    {
        x1 = topLeft.x;
        y1 = topLeft.y;
        x2 = bottomRight.x;
        y2 = bottomRight.y;
        return this;
    }
MyRect buildRect(Point topLeft, int w, int h)
    {
        x1 = topLeft.x;
        y1 = topLeft.y;
        x2 = (x1 + w);
        y2 = (y1 + h);
        return this;
    }
    void printRect(){
        System.out.print("MyRect: <" + x1 + ", " +
        y1);
        System.out.println(", " + x2 + ", " + y2 +
        ">");
    }
    public static void main(String args[]) {
        MyRect rect = new MyRect();
        System.out.println("Calling buildRect with
        coordinates 25,25 50,50:");
        rect.buildRect(25, 25, 50, 50);
        rect.printRect();
        System.out.println("Calling buildRect w/
        points (10,10), (20,20):");
        rect.buildRect(new Point(10,10), new
        Point(20,20));
        rect.printRect();
        System.out.print("Calling buildRect w/1
        point (10,10),");
        System.out.println(" width (50) and height
```

```
    (50)");
    rect.buildRect(new Point(10,10), 50, 50);
    rect.printRect();
  }
}
```

Output Generated

```
Calling buildRect with coordinates 25,25 50,50:
MyRect: <25, 25, 50, 50>
Calling buildRect w/points (10,10), (20,20):
MyRect: <10, 10, 20, 20>
Calling buildRect w/1 point (10,10), width (50) and
height (50)
MyRect: <10, 10, 60, 60>
```

As you can see from this example, all the buildRect() methods work based on the arguments with which they are called. You can define as many versions of a method as you need to in your own classes to implement the behavior you need for that class.

Constructor Methods

In addition to regular methods, you can also define constructor methods in your class definition. A ***constructor method*** is a special kind of method that determines how an object is initialized when it's created.

Unlike regular methods, you can't call a constructor method by calling it directly; instead, constructor methods are called by Java automatically. Here's how it works: when you use **new** to create a new instance of a class, Java does three things:

- Allocates memory for the object
- Initializes that object's instance variables, either to their initial values or to a default (0 for numbers, null for objects, false for booleans, '\0' for characters)
- Calls the class's constructor method (which may be one of several methods)

If a class doesn't have any special constructor methods defined, you'll still end up with an object, but you might have to set its instance variables or call other methods that object needs to initialize itself. All the examples you've created up to this point have behaved like this.

By defining constructor methods in your own classes, you can set initial values of instance variables, call methods based on those variables or call methods on other objects, or calculate initial properties of your object. You can also overload constructors, as you would regular methods, to create an object that has specific properties based on the arguments you give to new.

Basic Constructors

Constructors look a lot like regular methods, with two basic differences:

- Constructors always have the same name as the class.
- Constructors don't have a return type.

For example, the program below shows a simple class called Person, with a constructor that initializes its instance variables based on the arguments to new. The class also includes a method for the object to introduce itself, and a main() method to test each of these things.

// The Person class.

```
class Person {
    String name;
    int age;
    Person(String n, int a) {
        name = n;
        age = a;
    }
    void printPerson() {
       System.out.print("Hi, my name is " + name);
       System.out.println(". I am " + age + "
       years old.");
    }
    public static void main (String args[]) {
       Person p;
       p = new Person("Laura", 20);
       p.printPerson();
```

```
        p = new Person("Tommy", 3);
        p.printPerson();
    }
}
```

Output Generated

```
Hi, my name is Laura. I am 20 years old.
Hi, my name is Tommy. I am 3 years old.
```

Calling Another Constructor

Some constructors you write may be a superset of another constructor defined in your class; that is, they might have the same behavior plus a little bit more. Rather than duplicating identical behavior in multiple constructor methods in your class, it makes sense to be able to just call that first constructor from inside the body of the second constructor. Java provides a special syntax for doing this. To call a constructor defined on the current class, use this form:

```
this(arg1, arg2, arg3...);
```

The arguments to this are, of course, the arguments to the constructor.

Overloading Constructors

Like regular methods, constructors can also take varying numbers and types of parameters, enabling you to create your object with exactly the properties you want it to have, or for it to be able to calculate properties from different kinds of input.

For example, the buildRect() methods you defined in the MyRect class earlier today would make excellent constructors, because what they're doing is initializing an object's instance variables to the appropriate values. So, instead of the original buildRect() method you had defined (which took four parameters for the coordinates of the corners), you can create a constructor instead. The program below shows a new class, called MyRect2, that has all the same functionality of the original MyRect, except with overloaded constructor methods instead of the buildRect() method.

// The MyRect2 class (with constructors).

```
import java.awt.Point;
class MyRect2 {
   int x1 = 0;
   int y1 = 0;
   int x2 = 0;
   int y2 = 0;
   MyRect2(int x1, int y1, int x2, int y2) {
      this.x1 = x1;
      this.y1 = y1;
      this.x2 = x2;
      this.y2 = y2;
   }
   MyRect2(Point topLeft, Point bottomRight) {
      x1 = topLeft.x;
      y1 = topLeft.y;
      x2 = bottomRight.x;
      y2 = bottomRight.y;
   }
   MyRect2(Point topLeft, int w, int h) {
      x1 = topLeft.x;
      y1 = topLeft.y;
      x2 = (x1 + w);
      y2 = (y1 + h);
   }
   void printRect() {
      System.out.print("MyRect: <" + x1 + ", " +
      y1);
      System.out.println(", " + x2 + ", " + y2 +
      ">");
   }
   public static void main(String args[]) {
      MyRect2 rect;
      System.out.println("Calling MyRect2 with
      coordinates 25,25 50,50:");
      rect = new MyRect2(25, 25, 50,50);
      rect.printRect();
      System.out.println("Calling MyRect2 w/points
      (10,10), (20,20):");
      rect= new MyRect2(new Point(10,10), new
      Point(20,20));
      rect.printRect();
      System.out.print("Calling MyRect2 w/1 point
```

```
         (10,10),");
        System.out.println(" width (50) and height
         (50)");
        rect = new MyRect2(new Point(10,10), 50,
         50);
        rect.printRect();
    }
}
```

Output Generated

```
Calling MyRect2 with coordinates 25,25 50,50:
MyRect: <25, 25, 50, 50>
Calling MyRect2 w/points (10,10), (20,20):
MyRect: <10, 10, 20, 20>
Calling MyRect2 w/1 point (10,10), width (50) and
height (50)
MyRect: <10, 10, 60, 60>
```

Inheritance

Inheritance is one of the most crucial concepts in object-oriented programming, and it has a very direct effect on how you design and write your Java classes. Inheritance is a powerful mechanism that means when you write a class you only have to specify how that class is different from some other class; inheritance will give you automatic access to the information contained in that other class.

Each class has a superclass (the class above it in the hierarchy), and each class can have one or more subclasses (classes below that class in the hierarchy). Classes further down in the hierarchy are said to inherit from classes further up in the hierarchy.

Subclasses inherit all the methods and variables from their superclasses—that is, in any particular class, if the superclass defines behavior that your class needs, you don't have to redefine it or copy that code from some other class. Your class automatically gets that behavior from its superclass, that superclass gets behavior from its superclass, and so on all the way up the hierarchy. Your class becomes a combination of all the features of the classes above it in the hierarchy.

At the top of the Java class hierarchy is the class Object; all classes inherit from this one superclass. Object is the most general class in the hierarchy; it defines behavior inherited by all the classes in the Java class hierarchy. Each class farther down in the hierarchy adds more information and becomes more tailored to a specific purpose. In this way, you can think of a class hierarchy as defining very abstract concepts at the top of the hierarchy and those ideas becoming more concrete the farther down the chain of superclasses you go. This mechanism for defining new classes as the differences between them and their superclasses is called *subclassing*.

Subclassing involves creating a new class that inherits from some other class in the class hierarchy. Using subclassing, you only need to define the differences between your class and its parent; the additional behavior is all available to your class through inheritance.

Creating a Class Hierarchy

If you're creating a larger set of classes, it makes sense for your classes not only to inherit from the existing class hierarchy, but also to make up a hierarchy themselves. This may take some planning beforehand when you're trying to figure out how to organize your Java code, but the advantages are significant once it's done:

- When you develop your classes in a hierarchy, you can factor out information common to multiple classes in superclasses, and then reuse that superclass's information over and over again. Each subclass gets that common information from its superclass.
- Changing (or inserting) a class further up in the hierarchy automatically changes the behavior of the lower classes—no need to change or recompile any of the lower classes, because they get the new information through inheritance and not by copying any of the code.

How Inheritance Works

How does inheritance work? How is it that instances of one class can automatically get variables and methods from the classes further up in the hierarchy?

For instance variables, when you create a new instance of a class, you get a "slot" for each variable defined in the current class and for each variable defined in all its superclasses. In this way, all the classes combine to form a template for the current object and then each object fills in the information appropriate to its situation.

Methods operate similarly: new objects have access to all the method names of its class and its superclasses, but method definitions are chosen dynamically when a method is called. That is, if you call a method on a particular object, Java first checks the object's class for the definition of that method. If it's not defined in the object's class, it looks in that class's superclass, and so on up the chain until the method definition is found.

Overriding Methods

When you call a method on an object, Java looks for that method definition in the class of that object, and if it doesn't find one, it passes the method call up the class hierarchy until a method definition is found. Method inheritance enables you to define and use methods repeatedly in subclasses without having to duplicate the code itself.

However, there may be times when you want an object to respond to the same methods but have different behavior when that method is called. In this case, you can override that method. Overriding a method involves defining a method in a subclass that has the same signature as a method in a superclass. Then, when that method is called, the method in the subclass is found and executed instead of the one in the superclass.

Creating Methods that Override Existing Methods

To override a method, all you have to do is create a method in your subclass that has the same signature (name, return type, and parameter list) as a method defined by one of your class's superclasses. Because Java executes the first method definition it finds that matches the signature, this effectively "hides" the original method definition. Here's a simple example which shows a simple class with a method called printMe(), which prints out the name of the class and the values of its instance variables.

// The PrintClass class.

```
class PrintClass {
    int x = 0;
    int y = 1;
    void printMe() {
        System.out.println("X is " + x + ", Y is "
+ y);
        System.out.println("I am an instance of the
class " +
        this.getClass().getName());
    }
}
```

The program below shows a class called PrintSubClass that is a subclass of (extends) PrintClass. The only difference between PrintClass and PrintSubClass is that the latter has a z instance variable.

// The PrintSubClass class.

```
class PrintSubClass extends PrintClass {
    int z = 3;
    public static void main(String args[]) {
        PrintSubClass obj = new PrintSubClass();
        obj.printMe();
    }
}
```

Output Generated:

```
X is 0, Y is 1
```

I am an instance of the class PrintSubClass

In the main() method of PrintSubClass, you create a PrintSubClass object and call the printMe() method. Note that PrintSubClass doesn't define this method, so Java looks for it in each of PrintSubClass's superclasses—and finds it, in this case, in PrintClass. Unfortunately, because printMe() is still defined in PrintClass, it doesn't print the z instance variable.

Using Super to Call Superclass Constructors

A subclass can call the constructor of the super class by use of the following form of super:

Syntax of using super:

```
super( parameter- list )
```

Here, the parameter-list specifies any parameters needed by the constructor in the superclass. super() must always be the first statement executed inside the subclass's constructor.

```
// BoxWeight now uses super to initoaloze its box
attributes
class BoxWeight extends Box {
  double weight;

// initialize width, height and depth using super()
BoxWeight(double w, double h, double d , double m)
{
        Super(w,h,d);
        Weight=m;
   }
}
```

Here, BoxWeight calls super() with the parameters w,h,d. this causes the Box() constructor to be called, which initializes width, height, depth using these values.

Overriding Constructors

Constructors cannot technically be overridden. Because they always have the same name as the current class, you're always creating new constructors instead of inheriting the ones you've got. Much of the time, this is fine, because when your class's constructor is called, the constructor with the same signature for all your superclass is also called, so initialization of all the parts of a class you inherit can happen.

However, when you're defining constructors for your own class, you may want to change how your object is initialized, not only by initializing new variables your class adds, but also to change the contents of variables that are already there. You do this by explicitly calling your superclass's constructors, and then changing whatever you like.

Finalizer Methods

Finalizer methods are like the opposite of constructor methods; whereas a constructor method is used to initialize an object, finalizer methods are called just before the object is garbage-collected and its memory reclaimed.

The finalizer method is simply finalize(). The Object class defines a default finalizer method, which does nothing. To create a finalizer method for your own classes, override the finalize() method using this signature:

```
protected void finalize() {
    ...
}
```

Inside the body of that finalize() method, include any cleaning up you want to do for that object. You can also call super.finalize() to allow your class's superclasses to finalize your object, if necessary.

You can always call the finalize() method yourself at any time; it's just a plain method like any other. However, calling finalize() does not trigger an object to be garbage-collected. Only removing all references to an object will cause it to be marked for deleting.

Finalizer methods are best used for optimizing the removal of an object—for example, by removing references to other objects, by releasing external resources that have acquired, or for other behaviors that may make it easier for that object to be removed. In most cases, you will not need to use finalize() at all.

Java Applet Basics

Much of Java's current popularity has come about because of Java-capable World Wide Web browsers and their support for applets: small programs that run inside a Web page and can be used to create dynamic, interactive Web designs. Applets, are written in the Java language, and can be viewed in any browser that supports Java, including Sun's HotJava and Netscape's Navigator 2.0.

How Applets and Applications Are Different

In short, Java applications are stand-alone Java programs that can be run by using just the Java interpreter, for example, from a command line. Most everything you've used up to this point in the book has been a Java application, albeit a simple one.

Java applets, however, are run from inside a World Wide Web browser. A reference to an applet is embedded in a Web page using a special HTML tag. When a reader, using a Java-enabled browser, loads a Web page with an applet in it, the browser downloads that applet from a Web server and executes it on the local system (the one the browser is running on).

Because Java applets run inside a Java browser, they have the advantage of the structure the browser provides: an existing window, an event-handling and graphics context, and the surrounding user interface. Java applications can also create this structure, but they don't require it

The convenience that applets have over applications in terms of structure and UI capabilities, however, is hampered by restrictions on what applets can do. Given the fact that Java applets can be downloaded from anywhere and run on a client's system, restrictions are necessary to prevent an applet from causing system damage or security breaches. Without these restrictions in place, Java applets could be written to contain viruses or trojan horses (programs that seem friendly but do some sort of damage to the system), or be used to compromise the security of the system that runs them. The restrictions on what an applet can do include the following:

- Applets can't read or write to the reader's file system, except in specific directories (which are defined by the user through an access control list that, by default, is empty). Some browsers may not even allow an applet to read or write to the file system at all, or at the same time as using the network.
- Applets can't usually communicate with a server other than the one that had originally stored the applet. (This may be

configurable by the browser; however, you should not depend on having this behavior available.)

- Applets can't run any programs on the reader's system. For Unix systems, this includes forking a process.
- Applets can't load programs native to the local platform, including shared libraries such as DLLs.

In addition, Java itself includes various forms of security and consistency checking in the Java compiler and interpreter to prevent unorthodox use of the language. This combination of restrictions and security features make it more difficult for a rogue Java applet to do damage to the client's system.

Creating Applets

For the most part, all the Java programs you've created up to this point have been Java applications—simple programs with a single main() method that created objects, set instance variables, and ran methods.

To create an applet, you create a subclass of the class Applet, in the java.applet package. The Applet class provides behavior to enable your applet not only to work within the browser itself, but also to take advantage of the capabilities of AWT to include UI elements, to handle mouse and keyword events, and to draw to the screen. Although your applet can have as many "helper" classes as it needs, it's the main applet class that triggers the execution of the applet. That initial applet class always has a signature like this:

```
public class myClass extends java.applet.Applet {
    ...
}
```

Note the public keyword. Java requires that your applet subclass be declared public. Again, this is true only of your main applet class; any helper classes you create can be public or private as you wish.

When Java encounters your applet in a Web page, it loads your initial applet class over the network, as well as any other helper classes that first class uses. Unlike with applications, where Java calls the

main() method directly on your initial class, when your applet is loaded, Java creates an instance of that class, and a series of Applet methods are called on that instance. Different applets that use the same class use different instances, so each one can behave differently from the other applets running in the same browser.

Major Applet Activities

To create a basic Java application, your class has to have one method, **main()**, with a specific signature. Then, when your application starts up, **main()** is executed, and from main() you can set up the behavior that your program needs. Applets are similar but more complicated. Applets have many different activities that correspond to various major events in the life cycle of the applet—for example, initialization, painting, or mouse events. Each activity has a corresponding method, so when an event occurs, the browser or other Java-capable tool calls those specific methods.

The default implementations of these activity methods do nothing; to provide behavior for an event you must override the appropriate method in your applet's subclass. You don't have to override all of them, of course; different applet behavior requires different methods to be overridden.

The five of the more important methods in an applet's execution: initialization, starting, stopping, destroying, and painting.

Initialization

Initialization occurs when the applet is first loaded (or reloaded). Initialization might include creating the objects it needs, setting up an initial state, loading images or fonts, or setting parameters. To provide behavior for the initialization of your applet, override the init() method:

```
public void init() {
...
}
```

Starting

After an applet is initialized, it is started. Starting can also occur if the applet was previously stopped. For example, an applet is stopped if the reader follows a link to a different page, and it is started again when the reader returns to this page. Note that starting can occur several times during an applet's life cycle, whereas initialization happens only once. To provide startup behavior for your applet, override the start() method:

```
public void start() {
    ...
}
```

Functionality that you put in the start() method might include starting up a thread to control the applet, sending the appropriate messages to helper objects, or in some way telling the applet to begin running

Stopping

Stopping and starting go hand in hand. Stopping occurs when the reader leaves the page that contains a currently running applet, or you can stop the applet yourself by calling stop(). By default, when the reader leaves a page any threads the applet had started will continue running.

```
public void stop() {
    ...
}
```

Destroying

Destroying sounds more violent than it is. Destroying enables the applet to clean up after itself just before it is freed or the browser exits—for example, to kill any running threads or to release any other running objects. Generally, you won't want to override destroy() unless you have specific resources that need to be released—for example, threads that the applet has created. To provide clean up behavior for your applet, override the destroy() method:

```
public void destroy() {
    ...
}
```

Technical Note: How is destroy() different from finalize()? First, destroy() applies only to applets. finalize() is a more general-purpose way for a single object of any type to clean up after itself.

Painting

Painting is how an applet actually draws something on the screen, be it text, a line, a colored background, or an image. Painting can occur many hundreds of times during an applet's life cycle—for example, once after the applet is initialized, if the browser is placed behind another window on the screen and then brought forward again, if the browser window is moved to a different position on the screen, or perhaps repeatedly in the case of animations. You override the **paint()** method for your applet to have an actual appearance on the screen. The **paint()** method looks like this:

```
public void paint(Graphics g) {
    ...
}
```

Note that unlike the other major methods in this section, **paint()** takes an argument, an instance of the class Graphics. This object is created and passed to paint by the browser, so you don't have to worry about it. However, you will have to make sure that the Graphics class (part of the java.awt package) gets imported into your applet code, usually through an import statement at the top of your Java file:

```
import java.awt.Graphics;
```

A Simple Applet

// The Hello Again applet.

```
import java.awt.Graphics;
import java.awt.Font;
```

```
import java.awt.Color;
public class HelloAgainApplet extends
java.applet.Applet {
    Font f = new Font("TimesRoman", Font.BOLD,
    36);
    public void paint(Graphics g) {
      g.setFont(f);
      g.setColor(Color.red);
      g.drawString("Hello again!", 5, 50);
  }
}
```

This applet overrides paint(), one of the major methods described in the previous section. Because the applet doesn't actually do much (all it does is print a couple of words to the screen), and there's not really anything to initialize, you don't need a start() or a stop() or an init() method.

The paint method is where the real work of this applet (what little work goes on) really occurs. The Graphics object passed into the paint() method holds the graphics state—that is, the current features of the drawing surface. Lines 10 and 11 set up the font and color for this graphics state (here, the font object held in the f instance variable, and an object representing the color red that's stored in the Color class's variable red).

Line 12 then draws the string "Hello Again!" by using the current font and color at the position 5, 50. Note that the 0 point for x, y is at the top left of the applet's drawing surface, with positive y moving downward, so 50 is actually at the bottom of the applet

Including an Applet on a Web Page

After you create a class or classes that contain your applet and compile them into class files as you would any other Java program, you have to create a Web page that will hold that applet by using the HTML language. There is a special HTML tag for including applets in Web pages; Java-capable browsers use the information contained in that tag to locate the compiled class files and execute the applet itself. In this section, you'll learn about how to put Java applets in a Web page and how to serve those files to the Web at large.

The <APPLET> Tag

To include an applet on a Web page, use the <APPLET> tag. <APPLET> is a special extension to HTML for including applets in Web pages. The code below shows a very simple example of a Web page with an applet included in it.

A simple HTML page.

```
<APPLET CODE="HelloAgainApplet.class" WIDTH=200
HEIGHT=50>
</APPLET>
```

There are three things to note about the <APPLET> tag in this page:

- The CODE attribute indicates the name of the class file that contains this applet, including the .class extension. In this case, the class file must be in the same directory as this HTML file. To indicate applets are in a specific directory, use CODEBASE, described later today.
- WIDTH and HEIGHT are required and are used to indicate the bounding box of the applet—that is, how big a box to draw for the applet on the Web page. Be sure you set WIDTH and HEIGHT to be an appropriate size for the applet; depending on the browser, if your applet draws outside the boundaries of the space you've given it, you may not be able to see or get to those parts of the applet outside the bounding box.
- The text between the <APPLET> and </APPLET> tags is displayed by browsers that do not understand the <APPLET> tag (which includes most browsers that are not Java-capable). Because your page may be viewed in many different kinds of browsers, it is a very good idea to include alternate text here so that readers of your page who don't have Java will see something other than a blank line. Here, you include a simple statement that says There would be an applet here if your browser supported Java.

Simple Animation and Threads

The sort of simple animation takes only a few methods to implement in Java, but those few methods are the basis for any Java applet that you want to update the screen dynamically. Starting with simple animations is a good way to build up to more complicated applets. Specifically, you'll explore the following:

- How Java animations work—the paint() and repaint() methods, starting and stopping dynamic applets, and how to use and override these methods in your own applets
- Threads—what they are and how they can make your applets more well-behaved with other applets and with the Java system in general
- Reducing animation flicker, a common problem with animation in Java

Creating Animation in Java

Animation in Java involves two steps: constructing a frame of animation, and then asking Java to paint that frame. Repeat as necessary to create the illusion of movement. The basic, static applets that you created yesterday taught you how to accomplish the first part; all that's left is how to tell Java to paint a frame.

Painting and Repainting

The **paint()** method, as you learned yesterday, is called by Java whenever the applet needs to be painted—when the applet is initially drawn, when the window containing it is moved, or when another window is moved from over it. You can also, however, ask Java to repaint the applet at a time you choose. So, to change the appearance of what is on the screen, you construct the image or "frame" you want to paint, and then ask Java to paint this frame. If you do this repeatedly, and fast enough, you get animation inside your Java applet. That's all there is to it.

Where does all this take place? Not in the **paint()** method itself. All **paint()** does is put dots on the screen. **paint()**, in other words, is responsible only for the current frame of the animation. The real work of changing what **paint()** does, of modifying the frame for an animation, actually occurs somewhere else in the definition of your applet.

In that "somewhere else," you construct the frame (set variables for **paint()** to use, create Color or Font or other objects that **paint()** will need), and then call the **repaint()** method. **repaint()** is the trigger that causes Java to call paint() and causes your frame to get drawn.

Starting and Stopping an Applet's Execution

Remember start() and stop()? These are the methods that trigger your applet to start and stop running. With animations and other Java applets that are actually processing and running over time, you'll need to make use of start() and stop() to trigger the start of your applet's execution, and to stop it from running when you leave the page that contains that applet. For many applets, you'll want to override start and stop for just this reason.

The start() method triggers the execution of the applet. You can either do all the applet's work inside that method, or you can call other object's methods in order to do so. Usually, start() is used to create and begin execution of a thread so the applet can run in its own time.

The stop(), on the other hand, suspends an applet's execution so when you move off the page on which the applet is displaying, it doesn't keep running and using up system resources. Most of the time when you create a start() method, you should also create a corresponding stop().

Programming Techniques of JAVA

Program 1.

```
// program to add two numbers

class AddCommand
{
public static void main(String arr[])
{
int x;
int y;
x=Integer.parseInt(arr[0]);
y=Integer.parseInt(arr[1]);
System.out.println(x+y);
}
}
```

Program 2.

```
// program to add two numbers and store the result
in a textbox
import java.applet.*;
import java.awt.*;
import java.awt.event.*;
public class AddNumbers extends Applet implements
ActionListener
{
 TextField t1,t2,t3;
 Button b;
```

(Contd.)

```
public void init()
{
 t1=new TextField(15);
 t2=new TextField(15);
 t3=new TextField(15);
 b=new Button("ADD");
 add(b);
 add(t1);
 add(t2);
 add(t3);
 b.addActionListener(this);
 t1.addActionListener(this);
 t2.addActionListener(this);
 t3.addActionListener(this);
}
public void actionPerformed(ActionEvent ae)
 {
  String a;
  a=t1.getText();
  String c;
  c=t2.getText();
  int d=Integer.parseInt(a)+Integer.parseInt(c);
  t3.setText(new Integer(d).toString());
  repaint();
 }
public void paint(Graphics g)
 {
 }
}
```

Program 3.

```
import p1.*;
class b
{
 public static void main(String args[])
 {
  a a1=new a();
 }
}
```

Program 4.

```
//A java servlet doing JDBC

import java.io.*;
import javax.servlet.*;
import javax.servlet.http.*;
import java.sql.*;
public class Books extends HttpServlet
{
 Connection con;
 ResultSet rs;
 PrintWriter pw;
 Statement stm;
 String str;
 public void doGet(HttpServletRequest
req,HttpServletResponse res)throws
IOException,ServletException
  {
   doPost(req,res);
  }
 public void doPost(HttpServletRequest
req,HttpServletResponse res)throws
IOException,ServletException
  {
   pw=res.getWriter();
   res.setContentType("text/html");
   str=req.getParameter("t1");
    try
     {
     System.out.println("!!!!!!!!!!!!!!");

     Class.forName("sun.jdbc.odbc.JdbcOdbcDriver");
System.out.println("!!!!!!!!!!!!!!");
    con=DriverManager.getConnection("jdbc:odbc:books");
System.out.println("!!!!!!!!!!!!!!");
     stm=con.createStatement();
     rs=stm.executeQuery("Select * from Table1
where subject='"+str+"'");
     pw.println("<html><body><table>");
    System.out.println("Select * from Table1 where
subject='"+str+"'");
```

(Contd.)

```
     while(rs.next())
       {
       String str1=rs.getString(1);
       String str2=rs.getString(2);
       String str3=rs.getString(3);
    System.out.println(str1);
       pw.println("<tr><td>"+str1+"</
td><td>"+str2+"</td><td>"+str3+"</td></tr>");
       }
    pw.println("</table></body></html>");
    }
    catch(Exception e)
     {
      pw.println(e);
     }
   }
  }
```

Program 5.

```
// Demonstrate .
import java.awt.*;
import java.applet.*;
import java.util.*;

public class BorderLayoutDemo extends Applet {
  public void init() {
    setLayout(new BorderLayout());

    add(new Button("This is across the top."),
         BorderLayout.NORTH);
    add(new Label("The footer message might go
here."),
         BorderLayout.SOUTH);
    add(new Button("Right"), BorderLayout.EAST);
    add(new Button("Left"), BorderLayout.WEST);


    /*
    add(new TextField(12),BorderLayout.NORTH);
    add(new TextField(12),BorderLayout.EAST);
    add(new TextField(12),BorderLayout.WEST);
```

(Contd.)

```
    add(new TextField(12),BorderLayout.SOUTH);
     */

     /*
    add(new Checkbox(),BorderLayout.NORTH);
    add(new Checkbox(),BorderLayout.SOUTH);
     */

    String msg = "The reasonable man adapts " +
      "himself to the world;\n" +
      "the unreasonable one persists in " +
      "trying to adapt the world to himself.\n" +
      "Therefore all progress depends " +
      "on the unreasonable man.\n\n" +
      "        - George Bernard Shaw\n\n";

    add(new TextArea(msg), BorderLayout.CENTER);
   }
 }
```

Program 6.

```
// INHERITANCE

class BoxVolume
{
private int length;
private int width;
private int height;

public BoxVolume()
{
length=-1;
width=-1;
height=-1;
}

public BoxVolume(int l,int w,int h)
{
length=l;
width=w;
height=h;
}
```

(Contd.)

```
public int volume()
{
return length*width*height;
}
}

class BoxWeight extends BoxVolume
{
private float density;

public BoxWeight()
{
super();
density=-1;
}

public BoxWeight(int x,int y,int z,int d)
{
super(x,y,z);
density=d;
}

public float weight()
{
return density * volume();
}
}

class BoxDemo
{
public static void main(String args[])
{
BoxWeight bw=new BoxWeight(10,20,30,40);
float weight=bw.weight();
System.out.println(weight);
}
}
```

Program 7.

```
// program to make buttons

import java.applet.*;
```

(Contd.)

```
import java.awt.*;
import java.awt.event.*;
public class ButtonDemo extends Applet implements
ActionListener
{
 String str="";
 Button b1,b2,b3;
 public void init()
  {
   b1=new Button("one");
   b2=new Button("two");
   b3=new Button("three");
   add(b1);
   add(b2);
   add(b3);
   b1.addActionListener(this);
   b2.addActionListener(this);
   b3.addActionListener(this);
  }
 public void actionPerformed(ActionEvent ae)
  {
   str=ae.getActionCommand();
    repaint();
  }
 public void paint(Graphics g)
  {
  g.drawString("Button with label "+str+" pressed
",50,50);
  }
}
```

Program 8.

```
// program to make a calculator

import java.awt.*;
import java.applet.*;
import java.awt.event.*;
import javax.swing.*;

//defintion of the class calculator
public class Calculator extends Applet implements
```

(Contd.)

```
ActionListener
 {
  static final int row = 4,col=5;
  TextField t1;
  String text="";
  float result;
  Button b[]=new Button[20];
  String s[]={"7","8","9","/
","On","4","5","6","+","1/x","1",
        "2","3","-
","x^2","0","%","*","sqrt","Cancel"};
  int flag=0;
  int flg=0;
  Button eq=new Button(" = ");
  String str="";
  String str1="";
  String oper="";

  // init method
  public void init()
   {
    Panel p1=new Panel();    // making the first
panel
    // setting the layout of first panel
    p1.setLayout(new
FlowLayout(FlowLayout.CENTER));
    t1=new TextField(20);   // text box
    p1.add(t1);              //adding panel to
applet window
    Panel p2=new Panel(); //making the second
panel
    // setting the layout of second panel
   p2.setLayout(new GridLayout(row,col,40,20));
    setFont(new Font("SansSerif", Font.BOLD,
24));//setting the font

    // Exception handling
      try // the try block
   {
    for(int i=0;i<20;i++)
     {
     b[i]=new Button(s[i]);
```

(Contd.)

```
        p2.add(b[i]);
        }
     }
        catch(Exception e)
     {
      System.out.println(e);
     }//end of catch block

     // setting the layout of whole applet window
     setLayout(new BorderLayout());
     add(p1,BorderLayout.NORTH);   // adding panel
p1 to the north
     add(p2,BorderLayout.CENTER);  // adding panel
p2 in centre
     add(eq,BorderLayout.SOUTH);   // adding equals
button in the south
     eq.addActionListener(this);

     // adding buttons to action listener
     for(int i=0;i<s.length;i++)
     {
     b[i].addActionListener(this);
         }
 }

  // method actionPerformed of ActionListener
interface
  public void actionPerformed(ActionEvent ae)
    {

     Button temp=(Button)ae.getSource();//storing
references to buttons

        // checking whether operators are pressed or
operands
        if
(temp==b[3]||temp==b[8]||temp==b[9]||temp==b[13]||temp==b[14]

  ||temp==b[16]||temp==b[17]||temp==b[18]||temp==eq)
        {
     oper=temp.getLabel();

     // checking for the equals operator
```

(Contd.)

```
    if(oper.equals(" = "))
    {
      str1=text;
      if (flag==1)
        {

     result=Float.parseFloat(str)+Float.parseFloat(str1);
        }
      if (flag==2)
          result=Float.parseFloat(str)-
Float.parseFloat(str1);
      if (flag==3)

     result=Float.parseFloat(str)*Float.parseFloat(str1);
      if (flag==4)
       { try
          {
         if(str1.equals("0"))
           {
        JOptionPane.showMessageDialog(null,"Divide
by zero Error");
        t1.setText("");

           return;
           }
          else
           {
          result=Float.parseFloat(str)/
Float.parseFloat(str1);
           }
          }
         catch(Exception e)
          {
        System.out.println(e);
          }
       }
      if (flag==5)

     result=Float.parseFloat(str)*Float.parseFloat(str);
      if (flag==6)
          result=1/Float.parseFloat(str);
      if (flag==7)
```

(Contd.)

```
 result=Float.parseFloat(str)%Float.parseFloat(str1);
  // setting the value of result in the textbox
  t1.setText(""+result);
  str="";
  str1="";
  oper="";
  text=(new Float(result).toString());
}
  else
{
  oper=temp.getLabel();
  str=text;
  text="";

  //Trapping the operators
  if(oper.equals("+"))
    flag=1;
  if(oper.equals("-"))
    flag=2;
  if(oper.equals("*"))
    flag=3;
  if(oper.equals("/"))
    flag=4;
  if(oper.equals("x^2"))
    flag=5;
  if(oper.equals("1/x"))
    flag=6;
  if(oper.equals("%"))
    flag=7;

  // calculates square root
  if(oper.equals("sqrt"))

t1.setText(""+Math.sqrt((double)(Float.parseFloat(str))));
}
   }
   else
    {
     // trapping the numbers
     if (temp ==b[0])
       {
         text+="7";
       }
```

(Contd.)

```
 if (temp ==b[1])
  {
   text+="8";
  }
if (temp ==b[2])
  {
   text+="9";
  }
if (temp ==b[4])
  {
   text="0";
   flg=1;
  }
if (temp ==b[5])
  {
   text+="4";
  }
if (temp ==b[6])
  {
   text+="5";
  }
if (temp ==b[7])
  {
   text+="6";
  }
if (temp ==b[10])
  {
   text+="1";
  }
if (temp ==b[11])
  {
   text+="2";
  }
if (temp ==b[12])
  {
   text+="3";
  }
if (temp ==b[15])
  {
   text+="0";
  }
if (temp ==b[19])
  {
```

(Contd.)

```
            text+="";
           }
          t1.setText(text);
        }
     if(flg==1)
       {
         text="";
         flg=0;
       }
   }
    // paint method
    public void paint(Graphics g){}
   }// end of class
```

Program 9.

```
import p2.*;
class caller1
{
 caller1(callme ob1)
  {
  System.out.println(ob1.get_i());
  System.out.println(ob1.get_j());
  System.out.println(ob1.k);
  }
}
class caller2 extends callme
{
 caller2(callme ob1)
  {
  System.out.println(ob1.get_i());
  System.out.println(j);
  System.out.println(k);
  }
}
class caller3
{
 public static void main(String args[])
  {
  callme c=new callme();
  caller1 cr1=new caller1(c);
  caller2 cr2=new caller2(c);
}
}
```

Program 10.

```
class callme
{
  void call(String s)
  {
   System.out.print("["+s);
    try
     {
     Thread.sleep(500);
     }
   catch(InterruptedException e)
     {
     System.out.print(e);
     }
   System.out.println("]");
  }
}
```

Program 11.

```
// Demonstrate CardLayout.
import java.awt.*;
import java.awt.event.*;
import java.applet.*;

public class CardLayoutDemo extends Applet
  implements ActionListener, MouseListener {

  Checkbox Win98, winNT, solaris, mac;
  Panel osCards;
  CardLayout cardLO;
  Button Win, Other;

  public void init() {
    Win = new Button("Windows");
    Other = new Button("Other");
    add(Win);
    add(Other);

    cardLO = new CardLayout();
```

(Contd.)

```
osCards = new Panel();
osCards.setLayout(cardLO); // set panel layout
to card layout

Win98 = new Checkbox("Windows 98", null, true);
winNT = new Checkbox("Windows NT");
solaris = new Checkbox("Solaris");
mac = new Checkbox("MacOS");

// add Windows check boxes to a panel
Panel winPan = new Panel();
winPan.add(Win98);
winPan.add(winNT);

// Add other OS check boxes to a panel
Panel otherPan = new Panel();
otherPan.add(solaris);
otherPan.add(mac);

// add panels to card deck panel
osCards.add(winPan, "Windows");
osCards.add(otherPan, "Other");

// add cards to main applet panel
add(osCards);

// register to receive action events
Win.addActionListener(this);
Other.addActionListener(this);

// register mouse events
addMouseListener(this);
}

// Cycle through panels.
public void mousePressed(MouseEvent me) {
cardLO.next(osCards);
}

// Provide empty implementations for the other
MouseListener methods.
public void mouseClicked(MouseEvent me) {
}
```

(Contd.)

```
 public void mouseEntered(MouseEvent me) {
 }
 public void mouseExited(MouseEvent me) {
 }
 public void mouseReleased(MouseEvent me) {
 }

 public void actionPerformed(ActionEvent ae) {
   if(ae.getSource() == Win) {
     cardLO.show(osCards, "Windows");
   }
   else {
     cardLO.show(osCards, "Other");
   }
 }
}
```

Program 12.

```
// program to make check boxes

import java.applet.*;
import java.awt.*;
import java.awt.event.*;
public class CheckboxDemo extends Applet implements
ItemListener
{
 String str="";
 Checkbox cb1,cb2,cb3,cb4;
 public void init()
  {
   cb1=new Checkbox("Delhi");
   cb2=new Checkbox("Mumbai");
   cb3=new Checkbox("Chennai");
   cb4=new Checkbox();
   cb4.setLabel("Calcutta");
   add(cb1);
   add(cb2);
   add(cb3);
   add(cb4);
   cb1.addItemListener(this);
   cb2.addItemListener(this);
   cb3.addItemListener(this);
```

(Contd.)

```
   cb4.addItemListener(this);
   }
  public void itemStateChanged(ItemEvent ie)
   {
        repaint();
   }
  public void paint(Graphics g)
   {
    g.drawString(cb1.getLabel() + "selected" +
 cb1.getState(),10,60);
    g.drawString(cb2.getLabel() + "selected" +
 cb2.getState(),10,80);
    g.drawString(cb3.getLabel() + "selected" +
 cb3.getState(),10,100);
    g.drawString(cb4.getLabel() + "selected" +
 cb4.getState(),10,120);
   }
 }
```

Program 13.

```
// program to make combo box

import java.applet.*;
import java.awt.*;
import java.awt.event.*;
public class ChoiceDemo extends Applet implements
ItemListener
{
 Choice ch;
 public void init()
  {
   ch=new Choice();
   ch.add("Delhi");
   ch.add("Mumbai");
   ch.add("Chennai");
   ch.add("Calcutta");
   add(ch);
   ch.addItemListener(this);
  }
 public void itemStateChanged(ItemEvent ie)
  {
```

(Contd.)

```
        repaint();
    }
   public void paint(Graphics g)
    {
    g.drawString(ch.getSelectedItem(),10,60);
    }
}
```

Program 14.

```
// program to display random colours with their
codes

import java.awt.*;
import java.awt.event.*;
import java.applet.*;
import java.util.*;
public class choosecolors extends Applet implements
MouseListener
 {
   Random ran;
   public void init()
     {
     addMouseListener(this);
     }
   public void paint(Graphics g){}
   public void mouseClicked(MouseEvent me){}
   public void mousePressed(MouseEvent me)
     {
    ran=new Random();
    int r=Math.abs(ran.nextInt());
    int g=Math.abs(ran.nextInt());
    int b=Math.abs(ran.nextInt());
   showStatus("RED:"+r%256+"GREEN:"+g%256+"BLUE:"+b%256);
    setBackground(new Color(r%256,g%256,b%256));
     }
   public void mouseReleased(MouseEvent me){}
   public void mouseEntered(MouseEvent me){}
   public void mouseExited(MouseEvent me){}
}
```

Program 15.

```
// program for client

import java.io.*;
import java.net.*;
class ClientProgram
{
    public static void main(String args[])
    {
        try
        {
            Socket s=new Socket("192.168.0.45",8189);
            ObjectOutputStream oos=new
ObjectOutputStream
              (s.getOutputStream());
            BufferedReader br=new BufferedReader
              (new InputStreamReader(System.in));
            while(true)
            {
                String str=br.readLine();
                oos.writeObject(str);
                if(str.equalsIgnoreCase("bye"))
                    break;
            }
        }

        catch(Exception e)
        {
            System.out.println(e);
        }
    }
}
```

Program 16.

```
// program to create a simple thread

class CurrentThreadDemo
{
 public static void main(String s[])
   {
```

(Contd.)

```
Thread t=Thread.currentThread();
System.out.println("CurrentThread"+t);
t.setName("my Thread");
System.out.println("After name change"+t);
 try
  {
    for(int i=0;i<=5;i++)
     {
     System.out.println(i);
     Thread.sleep(1000);
     }
  }
 catch(InterruptedException e)
   {
    System.out.println(e);
   }
 }
}
```

Program 17.

```
class CurrentThreadDemo
{
 public static void main(String s[])
  {
  Thread t=Thread.currentThread();
  System.out.println("CurrentThread"+t);
  t.setName("my Thread");
  System.out.println("After name change"+t);
   try
    {
     for(int i=0;i<=5;i++)
      {
      System.out.println(i);
      Thread.sleep(1000);
      }
    }
   catch(InterruptedException e)
    {
     System.out.println(e);
    }
  }
 }
```

Program 18.

```
// program for the client to enter the sql query
through the client

import java.rmi.*;
import java.util.Vector;
import java.io.*;
public class DatabaseClient
{

public static void main(String args[])
{
Vector v;
BufferedReader br;
try
{
    String URL= "rmi://192.168.0.45/DBServer";

    DatabaseIntf
obj=(DatabaseIntf)Naming.lookup(URL);

    br=new BufferedReader(new
InputStreamReader(System.in));

    v=new Vector();

    int i;

    while(true)
    {
        v=null;
        System.out.println("Enter the SQL Query");
        String query=br.readLine();

        v=obj.sqlResults(query);

        Integer NUM_COL=(Integer)v.firstElement();
        int num_col=NUM_COL.intValue();
        for(i=1;i<=num_col;i++)
            System.out.print(v.elementAt(i)+"\t\t");
        System.out.println("");
```

(Contd.)

```
        Integer ROWS=(Integer)v.lastElement();
        int rows=ROWS.intValue();
        for(int j=1;j<=rows;j++)
        {
            for(int k=1;k<=num_col;k++)
            {

System.out.print(v.elementAt(i)+"\t\t");
                i++;
            }
            System.out.println("");

        }
    }
}
catch(Exception e){System.out.println(e);}
}
}
```

Program 19.

```
// interface for the sql query problem

import java.rmi.*;
import java.rmi.server.*;
import java.util.Vector;
import java.sql.*;
import java.net.*;

public class DatabaseIntfImpl extends
UnicastRemoteObject
  implements DatabaseIntf
{
Connection con;
Statement stm;
ResultSet rs;
ResultSetMetaData rsmd;
Vector v;
public DatabaseIntfImpl() throws RemoteException
{
    try
    {
```

(Contd.)

```
        System.out.println("Server Address : "
        +InetAddress.getLocalHost());

Class.forName("sun.jdbc.odbc.JdbcOdbcDriver");

con=DriverManager.getConnection("Jdbc:Odbc:supermarket");
        stm=con.createStatement();
    }
    catch(Exception e)
    {
        System.out.println(e);
    }
}

public Vector sqlResults (String query) throws
RemoteException
{
    int exp=0;
    try
    {
    int rows=0;
    v=new Vector();
    rs=stm.executeQuery(query);
    rsmd=rs.getMetaData();
    int num_col=(int)rsmd.getColumnCount();
    v.addElement(new Integer(num_col));

    for(int i=1;i<=num_col;i++)
    {
        v.addElement(rsmd.getColumnLabel(i));
    }

    while(rs.next())
    {
        for(int j=1;j<=num_col;j++)
        {
            v.addElement(rs.getString(j));

        }
        rows++;
    }

    v.addElement(new Integer(rows));
```

(Contd.)

```
        }
        catch(Exception e)
        {
            System.out.println(e);
            exp=1;
        }
        if(exp==0)
            return v;
        else
            return null;
    }
    }
```

Program 20.

```
// server program

import java.net.*;
import java.rmi.*;
public class DatabaseServer
{
public static void main(String args[])
{
try
{
      DatabaseIntfImpl obj=new DatabaseIntfImpl();
      Naming.rebind("DBServer",obj);
}
catch(Exception e)
{
    System.out.println("Exception: " + e);
}
}
}
```

Program 21.

```
// program for the visual environment which the
client will recieve

import java.rmi.*;
import java.util.Vector;
import java.io.*;
```

(Contd.)

```
import javax.swing.*;
import java.awt.*;
import java.awt.event.*;

class MyFrame extends Frame
{
    MyFrame(String title)
    {
        super(title);
        setSize(400,200);
        addWindowListener(new WindowAdapter(){
            public void windowClosing(WindowEvent we)
            {
                setVisible(false);
                System.exit(1);
            }
        });
    }
}

class DBClient extends JApplet
{
DBClient()
{
Vector v;
BufferedReader br;
try
{
    String URL= "rmi://192.168.0.45/DBServer";

    DatabaseIntf
obj=(DatabaseIntf)Naming.lookup(URL);

    br=new BufferedReader(new
InputStreamReader(System.in));

    v=new Vector();


    int i;

    String query=JOptionPane.showInputDialog("Enter
the SQL Query");
```

(Contd.)

```
    if(query==null)//if user presses cancel button
        System.exit(1);
    if(query.equals(""))//if user presses ok button
with blank string
        query="select * from table1";

    v=obj.sqlResults(query);//Invoking Remote Method
    if(v==null)//server will return null if query
fails
    {
        System.out.println("Exception Occured.Try
Again");
        System.exit(1);
    }

    Integer NUM_COL=(Integer)v.firstElement();
    int num_col=NUM_COL.intValue();
    String[] colHeads = new String[num_col];

    // Initialize column headings
    int vector_index=1;
    for(i=0;i<num_col;i++)
    {

colHeads[i]=(String)v.elementAt(vector_index);
        vector_index++;
    }


    Integer ROWS=(Integer)v.lastElement();
    int rows=ROWS.intValue();

    Object[][] data =new String[rows][num_col];

    //Allocate memory for table
    for(int j=0;j<rows;j++)
    {
        for(int k=0;k<num_col;k++)
        {

data[j][k]=(String)v.elementAt(vector_index);
            vector_index++;
        }
```

(Contd.)

```
    }

    // Get content pane
    Container contentPane = getContentPane();

    // Set layout manager
    contentPane.setLayout(new BorderLayout());

        // Create the table
    JTable table = new JTable(data, colHeads);


    int v1 =
ScrollPaneConstants.VERTICAL_SCROLLBAR_AS_NEEDED;
    int h1 =
ScrollPaneConstants.HORIZONTAL_SCROLLBAR_AS_NEEDED;

    JScrollPane jsp = new JScrollPane(table, v1,
h1);

    // Add scroll pane to the content pane
    contentPane.add(jsp, BorderLayout.CENTER);

    MyFrame mf=new MyFrame("RMI Results");
    // Add content pane to frame
    mf.add(contentPane);
    mf.setVisible(true);

}
catch(Exception e){System.out.println(e);}
}
}

public class DatabaseVisualClient
{
    public static void main(String args[])
    {
        new DBClient();
    }
}
```

Program 22.

```
// ASK USER A DATE & DISPLAY ITS RESPECTIVE DAY

import javax.swing.*;

class Day
{
public static void main(String args[])
{
int arr[]={31,28,31,30,31,30,31,31,30,31,30,31};
int month,date,year;
String _date,_year,_month;
_date=JOptionPane.showInputDialog(null,"ENTER THE
DATE");
_month=JOptionPane.showInputDialog(null,"ENTER THE
MONTH");
_year=JOptionPane.showInputDialog(null,"ENTER THE
YEAR");
date=Integer.parseInt(_date);
month=Integer.parseInt(_month);
year=Integer.parseInt(_year);
int  days=0;

 for(int i=1900;i<year;i++)
   {
      if((i%4==0 && i%100 !=0) || (i%100 ==0 &&
i%400 ==0))
            days=days+366;
      else
             days=days+365;

      if((i%4==0 && i%100 !=0) || (i%100 ==0 &&
i%400 ==0))
              arr[i]=29;
}
   for(int i=0;i<month-1;i++)
      days=days+arr[i];
      days=days+date;

        switch (days%7)
{
```

(Contd.)

```
        case 1:
            JOptionPane.showMessageDialog(null,"MONDAY");
              break;

        case 2:
            JOptionPane.showMessageDialog(null,"TUESDAY");
              break;

        case 3:
            JOptionPane.showMessageDialog(null,"WEDNESDAY");
              break;

        case 4:
            JOptionPane.showMessageDialog(null,"THURSDAY");
              break;

        case 5:
            JOptionPane.showMessageDialog(null,"FRIDAY");
              break;

        case 6:
            JOptionPane.showMessageDialog(null,"SATURDAY");
              break;

        case 0:
            JOptionPane.showMessageDialog(null,"SUNDAY");
              break;
    }
    System.exit(1);
    }
    }
```

Program 23.

```
// program to make dialog boxes

import java.applet.*;
import java.awt.*;
import java.awt.event.*;
class SampleDialog extends Dialog implements
ActionListener
{
 SampleDialog(Frame parent,String title)
```

(Contd.)

```
 {
 super(parent,title,false);
 setLayout(new FlowLayout());
 setSize(300,200);
 Label l=new Label("Press the button");
 add(l);
 Button b=new Button("Cancel");
 add(b);
 b.addActionListener(this);
 }
 public void actionPerformed(ActionEvent ae)
 {
  dispose();
 }
 public void paint(Graphics g)
 {
  g.drawString("This is a dialog box",10,80);
 }
}//end of class SampleDialog

class MenuFrame extends Frame implements
ActionListener
{
String msg=" ";
MenuFrame(String title)
{
 super(title);
 MenuBar mbar=new MenuBar();    //CREATING NEW
MENUBAR FOR FRAME//
 setMenuBar(mbar);      //Method of frame class//

//*CREATE THE 1st MENU ITEM *//

Menu figures=new Menu("Figures");
MenuItem item1,item2,item3,item4;
figures.add(item1=new MenuItem("line"));
figures.add(item2=new MenuItem("Rectangle"));
figures.add(item3=new MenuItem("oval"));
figures.add(item4=new MenuItem("DialogDemo"));
mbar.add(figures);      //Adding Menu to Menu Bar//
item1.addActionListener(this);
item2.addActionListener(this);
item3.addActionListener(this);
```

(Contd.)

```
item4.addActionListener(this);
addWindowListener(new WindowAdapter(){
public void windowClosing(WindowEvent me)
{
       setVisible(false);
}
});
}
public void actionPerformed(ActionEvent ae)
{
  String str=ae.getActionCommand();
       repaint();
 if(str.equals("DialogDemo"))
 {
  SampleDialog d=new SampleDialog(this,"My first
dailog box");
  d.setVisible(true);
 }
 else
  {
  msg=str;
  }
 repaint();
}
public void paint(Graphics g)
 {
  g.setColor(Color.blue);
  if(msg.equals("Rectangle"))
  g.fillRect(100,100,300,300);
  if(msg.equals("line"))
  g.drawLine(100,100,300,300);
  if(msg.equals("oval"))
  g.fillOval(100,100,300,300);
 }
}
public class DialogDemo extends Applet
{
 Frame f;
 public void init()
 {
  f=new MenuFrame("Drawing Dialog Box");
  int
```

(Contd.)

```
width=Integer.parseInt(getParameter("width"));
  int
height=Integer.parseInt(getParameter("height"));
 setSize(new Dimension(width,height));
 f.setSize(width,height);
 f.setVisible(true);
 }
 public void start()
 {
 f.setVisible(true);
 }
 public void stop()
 {
 f.setVisible(false);
 }
}
```

Program 24.

```
/* program to add two distances */

class Distance
{
  int feet;
  int inch;
  Distance()
   {
    feet=-1;
    inch=-1;
   }
   Distance(int f,int i)
   {
    feet=f;
    inch=i;
   }
  Distance add(Distance d)
   {
   Distance temp=new Distance();
   temp.feet=feet+d.feet;
   temp.inch=inch+d.inch;
   if(temp.inch>=12)
     {
      temp.feet+=1;
```

(Contd.)

```
        temp.inch-=12;

        }
       return temp;
      }
     void display()
       {
        System.out.println("Number of feets"+feet);
        System.out.println("Number of inches"+inch);
       }
    public static void main(String args[])
       {
        Distance d1=new Distance(5,12);
        Distance d2=new Distance(7,13);
        Distance d3=new Distance();
        d3=d1.add(d2);
        d3.display();
        }
}
```

Program 25.

```
// program to trap key events at the press of the
key

import java.awt.*;
import java.awt.event.*;
import java.applet.*;
public class Draw extends Applet implements
KeyListener
{
 String msg;
 public void init()
  {
  addKeyListener(this);
  requestFocus();
  }
 public void keyTyped(KeyEvent ke)
  {
  char ch=ke.getKeyChar();
  msg=msg+ch;
  repaint();
  }
```

(Contd.)

```
 public void keyPressed(KeyEvent ke){}
 public void keyReleased(KeyEvent ke){}
 public void paint(Graphics g)
  {
  g.drawString(msg,10,20);
  }
}
```

Program 26.

```
// a program of synchronization

class callme
{
 void call(string args[])
  {
  System.out.print("["+s);
try
{
Thread.sleep(500);
}
catch(InterruptedException e)
{
  System.out.print(e);
}
  System.out.println("]");
}
}
class caller implements Runnable
{
string msg;
Thread t;
callme c;
caller(callme temp,string s)
{
msg=s;
c=temp;
t=new Thread(this);
t.start();
}
public void run()
{
```

(Contd.)

```
c.call(msg);
}
}
class syncdemo
{
public static void main(String args{})
{
callme c=new callme();
caller obj1=new caller(c,"hello");
caller obj2=new caller(c,"synchronized");
caller obj3=new caller(c,"world");
try
{
obj1.t.join();
obj2.t.join();
obj3.t.join();
}
catch(InterruptedException e)
{
  System.out.print(e);
}
}
}
```

Program 27.

```
//EXCEPTIONAL HANDLING

class ExceptionDemo
{
  public static void main(String args[])
  {
   for(int i=-5;i<=5;i++)
   {
    try
     {
      System.out.println(10/i);
     }
    catch(Exception e)
    {
    System.out.println(e);
    System.out.println("ILLEGAL DIVISION BY
ZERO");
```

(Contd.)

```
      }
     }          //terminating for loop
   }
}

ding buttons to action listener
    for(int i=0;i<s.length;i++)
    {
    b[i].addActionListener(this);
        }
 }

  // method actionPerformed of ActionListener
interface
  public void actionPerformed(ActionEvent ae)
    {

     Button temp=(Button)ae.getSource();//storing
references to buttons

  // checking whether operators are pressed or
operands
       if
(temp==b[3]||temp==b[8]||temp==b[9]||temp==b[13]||temp==b[14]

  ||temp==b[16]||temp==b[17]||temp==b[18]||temp==eq)
       {
    oper=temp.getLabel();

    // checking for the equals operator
    if(oper.equals(" = "))
    {
      str1=text;
      if (flag==1)
        {

     result=Float.parseFloat(str)+Float.parseFloat(str1);
        }
      if (flag==2)
          result=Float.parseFloat(str)-
Float.parseFloat(str1);
      if (flag==3)
```

(Contd.)

```
        result=Float.parseFloat(str)*Float.parseFloat(str1);
         if (flag==4)
          { try
             {
            if(str1.equals("0"))
              {
          JOptionPane.showMessageDialog(null,"Divide
by zero Error");
          t1.setText("");

              return;
              }
             else
              {
           result=Float.parseFloat(str)/
Float.parseFloat(str1);
              }
             }
           catch(Exception e)
             {
         System.out.println(e);
             }
          }
        if (flag==5)

       result=Float.parseFloat(str)*Float.parseFloat(str);
        if (flag==6)
            result=1/Float.parseFloat(str);
        if (flag==7)

       result=Float.parseFloat(str)%Float.parseFloat(str1);
        // setting the value of result in the textbox
        t1.setText(""+result);
        str="";
        str1="";
        oper="";
        text=(new Float(result).toString());
      }
        else
      {
        oper=temp.getLabel();
        str=text;
        text="";
```

(Contd.)

```
//Trapping the operators
if(oper.equals("+"))
  flag=1;
if(oper.equals("-"))
  flag=2;
if(oper.equals("*"))
  flag=3;
if(oper.equals("/"))
  flag=4;
if(oper.equals("x^2"))
  flag=5;
if(oper.equals("1/x"))
  flag=6;
if(oper.equals("%"))
  flag=7;

// calculates square root
if(oper.equals("sqrt"))

t1.setText(""+Math.sqrt((double)(Float.parseFloat(str))));
 }
   }
   else
    {
     // trapping the numbers
     if (temp ==b[0])
      {
        text+="7";
      }
      if (temp ==b[1])
      {
        text+="8";
      }
     if (temp ==b[2])
      {
        text+="9";
      }
     if (temp ==b[4])
      {
        text="0";
        flg=1;
      }
     if (temp ==b[5])
```

(Contd.)

```
          {
            text+="4";
          }
        if (temp ==b[6])
          {
            text+="5";
          }
        if (temp ==b[7])
          {
            text+="6";
          }
        if (temp ==b[10])
          {
            text+="1";
          }
        if (temp ==b[11])
          {
            text+="2";
          }
        if (temp ==b[12])
          {
            text+="3";
          }
        if (temp ==b[15])
          {
            text+="0";
          }
        if (temp ==b[19])
          {
            text+="";
          }
         t1.setText(text);
      }
   if(flg==1)
    {
      text="";
      flg=0;
    }
 }
  // paint method
  public void paint(Graphics g){}
 }// end of class
```

Program 28.

```
//Run time polymorphism

class Figure
{
double dim1,dim2;
    Figure(double d1,double d2)
     {
      dim1=d1;
      dim2=d2;
     }
    double area()
     {
     System.out.println("AREA OF FIGURE CALLED");
      return -1;
     }
}

class Rectangle extends Figure
{
    Rectangle(double f1,double f2)
     {
       super(f1,f2);
     }
       double area()
        {
         System.out.println("AREA OF RECTANGLE
CALLED");
         return (dim1*dim2);
        }
}

class Triangle extends Figure
{
    Triangle(double f1,double f2)
      {
       super(f1,f2);
      }
     double area()
      {
       System.out.println("AREA OF TRIANGLE
CALLED");
```

(Contd.)

```
      return (0.5 * dim1 * dim2);
    }

 }

 class FigureDemo
 {
   public static void main(String s[])
    {
     Figure f;
     f=new Triangle(2,1);
    System.out.println(f.area());
     f=new Rectangle(4,10.5);
    System.out.println(f.area());
    }
 }
```

Program 29.

```
// Demonstrate a file dialog box

import java.awt.*;
import java.awt.event.*;

class SampleFrame extends Frame
{
 SampleFrame(String title)
  {
   super(title);
  MyWindowAdapter adapter=new
MyWindowadapter(this);
  addWindowListener(adapter);
  }
}

class MyWindowAdapter extends WindowAdapter
{
 Sampleframe sframe;
 public MyWindowadapter(SampleFrame sframe)
  {
  this .sframe=sframe;
  }
```

(Contd.)

```
 public void windowClosing(WindowEvent we)
  {
  sframe.setVisible(false);
  }
}

class FileDialogDemo1
{
 public static void main(String args[])
  {
    Frame f=new sframe("File dialog demo");
    f.setVisible(true);
    f.setSize(100,100);
    FileDialog fd=new FileDialog(f,"file dialog");
    fd.setVisible(true);
  }
}
```

Program 30.

```
// program to read from a file

import java.io.*;
class FileReaderDemo
{
 public static void main(String args[])
  {
    try
     {
      FileReader fr=new FileReader(args[0]);
      BufferedReader br=new BufferedReader(fr);
       String s;
      while((s=br.readLine())!=null)
        {
         System.out.println(s);
        }
       fr.close();
     }
    catch(Exception e)
     {
     System.out.println(e);
     }
   }
}
```

Program 31.

```
// program to write in a file

import java.io.*;
class FileWriterDemo
 {
  public static void main(String args[])
   {
    try
     {
       String str="";
       char buffer[];
      BufferedReader br=new BufferedReader(new
InputStreamReader(System.in));
      FileWriter fw=new FileWriter("mca.txt");
       while(true)
         {
          str=br.readLine();
          if(str.equalsIgnoreCase("stop"))
             break;
           str+="\n";
           buffer=new char[str.length()];
           str.getChars(0,str.length(),buffer,0);
           fw.write(buffer);
          }
        fw.close();
       }
       catch(Exception e)
          {
          System.out.println(e);
          }
     }
}
```

Program 32.

```
// program to show the use of final keyword

class FinalVar
{
  final int i;
  FinalVar(int x)
```

(Contd.)

```
   {
    i=x;
   }
  void display()
   {
   System.out.println(i);
   }
  public static void main(String args[])
   {
    FinalVar a=new FinalVar(10);
    a.display();
   }
 }
```

Program 33.

```
// Use left-aligned flow layout.
import java.awt.*;
import java.awt.event.*;
import java.applet.*;
/*
<applet code="FlowBorderLayoutDemo" width=250
height=200>
</applet>
*/

public class FlowBorderLayoutDemo extends Applet
  implements ItemListener {

  String msg = "";
  Checkbox Win98, winNT, solaris, mac;

  public void init() {
    //set left-aligned flow layout
   setLayout(new FlowLayout(FlowLayout.CENTER));

    Win98 = new Checkbox("Windows 98", null, true);
    winNT = new Checkbox("Windows NT");
    solaris = new Checkbox("Solaris");
    mac = new Checkbox("MacOS");

    add(Win98);
    add(winNT);
```

(Contd.)

```
    add(solaris);
    add(mac);

    // register to receive item events
    Win98.addItemListener(this);
    winNT.addItemListener(this);
    solaris.addItemListener(this);
    mac.addItemListener(this);


    setLayout(new BorderLayout());

    add(new Button("This is across the top."),
        BorderLayout.NORTH);
    add(new Label("The footer message might go
here."),
        BorderLayout.SOUTH);
    add(new Button("Right"), BorderLayout.EAST);
    add(new Button("Left"), BorderLayout.WEST);

    String msg = "The reasonable man adapts " +
      "himself to the world;\n" +
      "the unreasonable one persists in " +
      "trying to adapt the world to himself.\n" +
      "Therefore all progress depends " +
      "on the unreasonable man.\n\n" +
      "        - George Bernard Shaw\n\n";

    add(new TextArea(msg), BorderLayout.CENTER);
  }

  // Repaint when status of a check box changes.
  public void itemStateChanged(ItemEvent ie) {
    repaint();
  }

  // Display current state of the checkboxes.
  public void paint(Graphics g) {
    msg = "Current state: ";
    g.drawString(msg, 6, 80);
    msg = "  Windows 98: " + Win98.getState();
    g.drawString(msg, 6, 100);
    msg = "  Windows NT: " + winNT.getState();
```

(Contd.)

```
    g.drawString(msg, 6, 120);
    msg = "  Solaris: " + solaris.getState();
    g.drawString(msg, 6, 140);
    msg = "  Mac: " + mac.getState();
    g.drawString(msg, 6, 160);
  }
}
```

Program 34.

```
// Use left-aligned flow layout.
import java.awt.*;
import java.awt.event.*;
import java.applet.*;
/*
 <applet code="FlowLayoutDemo" width=250
height=200>
 </applet>
*/

public class FlowLayoutDemo extends Applet
  implements ItemListener {

  String msg = "";
  Checkbox Win98, winNT, solaris, mac;

  public void init() {
    // set left-aligned flow layout
   setLayout(new FlowLayout(FlowLayout.CENTER));

    Win98 = new Checkbox("Windows 98", null, true);
    winNT = new Checkbox("Windows NT");
    solaris = new Checkbox("Solaris");
    mac = new Checkbox("MacOS");


    add(Win98);
    add(winNT);
    add(solaris);
    add(mac);

    // register to receive item events
   Win98.addItemListener(this);
```

(Contd.)

```
    winNT.addItemListener(this);
    solaris.addItemListener(this);
    mac.addItemListener(this);
  }

  // Repaint when status of a check box changes.
  public void itemStateChanged(ItemEvent ie) {
    repaint();
  }

  // Display current state of the checkboxes.
  public void paint(Graphics g) {
    msg = "Current state: ";
    g.drawString(msg, 6, 80);
    msg = "  Windows 98: " + Win98.getState();
    g.drawString(msg, 6, 100);
    msg = "  Windows NT: " + winNT.getState();
    g.drawString(msg, 6, 120);
    msg = "  Solaris: " + solaris.getState();
    g.drawString(msg, 6, 140);
    msg = "  Mac: " + mac.getState();
    g.drawString(msg, 6, 160);
  }
}
```

Program 35.

```
// program to implement freehand drawing

import java.awt.*;
import java.awt.event.*;
import java.applet.*;
public class freehand extends Applet implements
MouseListener,MouseMotionListener
{
 int x1,y1,x2,y2;
int x[]=new int[1000];
int y[]=new int[1000];
int i=0;
Graphics g;
int flag=0;
 public void init()
  {
```

(Contd.)

```
    addMouseListener(this);
    addMouseMotionListener(this);
    requestFocus();
 g=getGraphics();
  }
 public void mousePressed(MouseEvent me)
   {
   }
 public void mouseClicked(MouseEvent me){}
 public void mouseReleased(MouseEvent me){}
 public void mouseEntered(MouseEvent me){}
 public void mouseExited(MouseEvent me){}
 public void mouseMoved(MouseEvent me){}
 public void mouseDragged(MouseEvent me)
   {
  if(flag==0)
{
   x1=x[i]=me.getX();
   y1=y[i]=me.getY();
  flag=1;
}
else
 {
      x2=x[i]=me.getX();
   y2=y[i]=me.getY();
  flag=0;
   g.drawLine(x1,y1,x2,y2);
   }
  i++;
}
 public void paint(Graphics g1)
 {
    for(int j=0;j<i-1;j++)
        g1.drawLine(x[j],y[j],x[j+1],y[j+1]);
 }
}
```

Program 36.

```
// program to say hello

import javax.swing.*;
class Greet
{
```

(Contd.)

```
  public static void main(String args[])
    {
     String name=null;
    name=JOptionPane.showInputDialog(null,"Enter
u'r name");
    JOptionPane.showMessageDialog(null,"Hello
"+name);
     System.exit(1);
    }
}
```

Program 37.

```
// Demonstrate GridLayout
import java.awt.*;
import java.applet.*;
/*
<applet code="GridLayoutDemo" width=300 height=200>
</applet>
*/

public class GridLayoutDemo extends Applet {
  static final int n = 4;
  public void init() {
setLayout(new FlowLayout(FlowLayout.RIGHT));
    add(new TextField(20));
    setLayout(new GridLayout(n, n));

    setFont(new Font("SansSerif", Font.BOLD, 24));

     for(int i = 0; i < n; i++) {
       for(int j = 0; j < n; j++) {
         int k = i * n + j;
         if(k > 0)
           add(new Button("" + k));
       }
     }
   }
}
```

Program 38.

```
class MultipleCatch
{
 public static void main(String args[])
  {
    int x=args.length;
    int y=10;
    try
     {
       int z=y/x;
       System.out.println(z);
       int arr[]={1,2,3,4};
       arr[30]=10;
      System.out.println("array testing");
     }
     catch(ArithmeticException e)
      {
       System.out.println(e);
      }
     catch(ArrayIndexOutOfBoundException e)
      {
       System.out.println(e);
      }
  }
```

Program 39.

```
// Demonstrate BorderLayout with insets.
import java.awt.*;
import java.applet.*;
import java.util.*;
/*
<applet code="InsetsDemo" width=400 height=200>
</applet>
*/

public class InsetsDemo extends Applet {
  public void init() {
    // set background color so insets can be easily
seen
    setBackground(Color.cyan);
```

(Contd.)

```
    setLayout(new BorderLayout());

    add(new Button("This is across the top."),
        BorderLayout.NORTH);
    add(new Label("The footer message might go
here."),
        BorderLayout.SOUTH);
    add(new Button("Right"), BorderLayout.EAST);
    add(new Button("Left"), BorderLayout.WEST);

    String msg = "The reasonable man adapts " +
      "himself to the world;\n" +
      "the unreasonable one persists in " +
      "trying to adapt the world to himself.\n" +
      "Therefore all progress depends " +
      "on the unreasonable man.\n\n" +
      "        - George Bernard Shaw\n\n";

    add(new TextArea(msg), BorderLayout.CENTER);
  }

  // add insets
  public Insets getInsets() {
    return new Insets(10, 10, 10, 10);
  }
}
```

Program 40.

```
import java.awt.*;
import java.awt.event.*;
import javax.swing.*;

public class JButtonDemo extends JApplet
implements ActionListener {
  JTextField jtf;

  public void init() {

    // Get content pane
    Container contentPane = getContentPane();
    contentPane.setLayout(new FlowLayout());
```

(Contd.)

```
    // Add buttons to content pane
    ImageIcon scissor = new
ImageIcon("Scissors.gif");
    JButton jb = new JButton(scissor);
    jb.setActionCommand("scissor");
    jb.addActionListener(this);
    contentPane.add(jb);

    ImageIcon phone = new ImageIcon("Phone.gif");
    jb = new JButton(phone);
    jb.setActionCommand("phone");
    jb.addActionListener(this);
    contentPane.add(jb);

    ImageIcon target = new ImageIcon("Target.gif");
    jb = new JButton(target);
    jb.setActionCommand("target");
    jb.addActionListener(this);
    contentPane.add(jb);

    ImageIcon family = new
ImageIcon("MyFamily.gif");
    jb = new JButton(family);
    jb.setActionCommand("family");
    jb.addActionListener(this);
    contentPane.add(jb);

    // Add text field to content pane
    jtf = new JTextField(15);
    contentPane.add(jtf);
  }

  public void actionPerformed(ActionEvent ae) {
    jtf.setText(ae.getActionCommand());
  }
}
```

Program 41.

```
import java.awt.*;
import javax.swing.*;
/*<applet code="JLabelDemo" width=660 height=450>
</applet>*/
```

(Contd.)

```
public class JLabelDemo extends JApplet {

  public void init() {
    // Get content pane
    Container contentPane = getContentPane();

    // Create an icon
    ImageIcon i1 = new ImageIcon("Share.gif");

    // Create a label
    JLabel jl = new JLabel("My Folder", i1,
JLabel.CENTER);

    // Add label to the content pane
    contentPane.add(jl);
  }
}
```

Program 42.

```
// Demonstrate scrollbar using swings

import java.awt.*;
import javax.swing.*;
public class JScrollPaneDemo extends JApplet
{
 public void init()
 {
 Container contentPane=getContentPane();
 contentPane.setLayout(new BorderLayout());
 JPanel jp=new JPanel();
 jp.setLayout(new GridLayout(20,20));
 int b=0;
 for(int i=0;i<20;i++)
  {
   for(int j=0;j<20;j++)
    {
    jp.add(new JButton("Button "+b));
     b++;
    }
  }
 int
```

(Contd.)

```
v=ScrollPaneConstants.VERTICAL_SCROLLBAR_AS_NEEDED;
 int
h=ScrollPaneConstants.HORIZONTAL_SCROLLBAR_AS_NEEDED;
 JScrollPane jsp=new JScrollPane(jp,v,h);
 // add scrollpane to content pane
 contentPane.add(jsp,BorderLayout.CENTER);
 }
}
```

Program 43.

```
// Demonstrate scrollbar using swings

import java.awt.*;
import javax.swing.*;
public class JTableDemo extends JApplet
{
 public void init()
 {
 Container contentPane=getContentPane();
 contentPane.setLayout(new BorderLayout());
 final String[] colheads={"Name","Phone no.","fax
no."};
 final Object[][] data={{"Abc","56789","3467"},
                        {"def","34567","7235"},
                        {"xyz","57584","6575"}};
 JTable jt=new JTable(data,colheads);
 int
v=ScrollPaneConstants.VERTICAL_SCROLLBAR_AS_NEEDED;
 int
h=ScrollPaneConstants.HORIZONTAL_SCROLLBAR_AS_NEEDED;
 JScrollPane jsp=new JScrollPane(jt,v,h);
 // add scrollpane to content pane
 contentPane.add(jsp,BorderLayout.CENTER);
 }
}
```

Program 44.

```
// program to make a linked list

import java.io.*;
import javax.swing.*;
```

(Contd.)

```
class LinkedList
 {
  private static LinkedList start=null;
  private int info;
  private LinkedList next;
  public void insert(int data)
    {
     if(start==null)
       {
        start=new LinkedList();
        start.info=data;
        start.next=null;
        return ;
       }
     LinkedList temp=start;
     while(temp.next!=null)
       {
        temp=temp.next;
       }
     temp.next=new LinkedList();
     temp=temp.next;
     temp.info=data;
     temp.next=null;
    }
  public void display()
    {
     LinkedList temp;
     temp=start;
     while(temp!=null)
       {
       System.out.println(temp.info);
        temp=temp.next;
       }
    }
  public static void main(String args[])
    {
      String data;
      BufferedReader br;
      br=new BufferedReader(new
InputStreamReader(System.in));
      LinkedList ob=new LinkedList();
      try
```

(Contd.)

```
        {
         while((data=br.readLine())!=null)
             {
                ob.insert(Integer.parseInt(data));
              }
        }
     catch(IOException e)
       {
        System.out.println(e);
       }
    ob.display();
 }
}
```

Program 45.

```
class Priority implements Runnable
{
 Thread t;
 boolean flag=true;
 long count=0;
 Priority(int p)
 {
  t=new Thread(this);
  t.setPriority(p);
 }
 public void start()
  {
   t.start();
  }
 public void stop()
  {
   flag=false;
  }
 public void run()
  {
   while(flag)
    count++;
  }
}
class Lowhigh
{
  public static void main(String args[])
```

(Contd.)

```
    {
   Thread.currentThread().setPriority(Thread.MAX_PRIORITY);
    Priority hi=new Priority(Thread.NORM_PRIORITY);
    Priority low=new
Priority(Thread.NORM_PRIORITY);
    hi.start();
    low.start();
    try
      {
      Thread.sleep(10000);
      }
    catch(Exception e)
      {
       System.out.println(e);
      }
    hi.stop();
    low.stop();
    try
      {
      hi.t.join();
      low.t.join();
      }
    catch(Exception e)
      {
      System.out.println(e);
      }
   System.out.println("Hi priority"+hi.count);
   System.out.println("Low priority"+low.count);
   }
}
```

Program 46.

```
/* program to calculate maximum of given 10 numbers */
import javax.swing.*;
class Maximum
{
  public static void main(String args[])
    {
      int arr[]=new int[20];
     int n=JOptionPane.showInputDialog(null,"How
many numbers?");
      for(int i=0;i<n;i++)
```

(Contd.)

```
     {
     arr[i]=JOptionPane.showInputDialog(null,"enter
the number?");
     }
     int max=arr[0];
   for(int i=1;i<arr.length;i++)
     {
       if(arr[i]>max)
           max=arr[i];
     }
    System.out.println(max);
  }
}
```

Program 47.

```
import java.applet.*;
import java.awt.*;
import java.awt.event.*;

class MenuFrame extends Frame implements
ActionListener,MouseMotionListener
{
 String str=" ";
 int x1,y1,x2,y2;
 int x[]=new int[1000];
 int y[]=new int[1000];
 int i=0;
 int flag=0;
 Graphics g1;
 MenuFrame(String title)
 {
  super(title);
  MenuBar mbar=new MenuBar();      //CREATING NEW
MENUBAR FOR FRAME//
  setMenuBar(mbar);               //Method of frame
class//

  //*CREATE THE 1st MENU ITEM *//

 Menu figures=new Menu("Figures");
 MenuItem item1,item2,item3,item4;
 figures.add(item1=new MenuItem("line"));
```

(Contd.)

```
figures.add(item2=new MenuItem("Rectangle"));
figures.add(item3=new MenuItem("oval"));
figures.add(item4=new MenuItem("Free Hand"));
mbar.add(figures);     //Adding Menu to Menu Bar//
item1.addActionListener(this);
item2.addActionListener(this);
item3.addActionListener(this);
item4.addActionListener(this);

// CREATE THE 2nd MENU ITEM*//
Menu colors=new Menu("colors");
MenuItem item5,item6,item7;
figures.add(item5=new MenuItem("Red"));
figures.add(item6=new MenuItem("Green"));
figures.add(item7=new MenuItem("Blue"));
mbar.add(colors);               //Adding Menu to
Menu Bar//
item5.addActionListener(this);
item6.addActionListener(this);
item7.addActionListener(this);*/

addWindowListener(new WindowAdapter(){
 public void windowClosing(WindowEvent me)
   {
       setVisible(false);
   }
  });
 }

public void actionPerformed(ActionEvent ae)
 {
 str=ae.getActionCommand();
 repaint();
 }
public void mouseDragged(MouseEvent me)
   {
   g1=getGraphics();
  if(flag==0)
{
   x1=x[i]=me.getX();
   y1=y[i]=me.getY();
  flag=1;
```

(Contd.)

```
}
else
 {
     x2=x[i]=me.getX();
   y2=y[i]=me.getY();
  flag=0;
   g1.drawLine(x1,y1,x2,y2);
    }
  i++;
}
 public void mouseMoved(MouseEvent me){}
 public void paint(Graphics g)
 {
  g.setColor(Color.blue);
  if(str.equals("Rectangle"))
  g.fillRect(100,100,300,300);
  if(str.equals("line"))
  g.drawLine(100,100,300,300);
  if(str.equals("oval"))
  g.fillOval(100,100,300,300);
  if(str.equals("Free Hand"))
    {
        for(int j=0;j<i-1;j++)
    g.drawLine(x[j],y[j],x[j+1],y[j+1]);
    }

  }

 }

public class MenuFigures extends Applet
{
Frame f;

public void init()
{
System.out.println("#############");
f=new MenuFrame("Drawing figures using Menu");
int width=Integer.parseInt(getParameter("width"));
int
height=Integer.parseInt(getParameter("height"));
setSize(new Dimension(width,height));
f.setSize(width,height);
```

(Contd.)

```
f.setVisible(true);
}
public void start()
{
  f.setVisible(true);
}
public void stop()
{
 f.setVisible(false);
}
}
```

Program 48.

```
// creating a simple program

import java.applet.*;
import java.awt.*;
import java.awt.event.*;

class MenuFrameDemo extends Frame implements
ActionListener
{
 String str=" ";
MenuFrameDemo()
{
}
MenuFrameDemo(String title)
{
 super(title);
 MenuBar mbar=new MenuBar();     //CREATING NEW
MENUBAR FOR FRAME//
 //MyWindowAdapter adapter=new
MyWindowAdapter(this);
 //addWindowListener(adapter);
 setMenuBar(mbar);              //Method of frame
class//

//*CREATE THE 1st MENU ITEM *//

Menu file=new Menu("File");
MenuItem item1,item2,item3,item4;
```

(Contd.)

```
file.add(item1=new MenuItem("New"));
file.add(item2=new MenuItem("Open"));
file.add(item3=new MenuItem("Save"));
file.add(item4=new MenuItem("SaveAs..."));
mbar.add(file);                    //Adding Menu to Menu
Bar//
item1.addActionListener(this);
item2.addActionListener(this);
item3.addActionListener(this);
item4.addActionListener(this);

//*CREATE THE 2nd MENU ITEM*//
Menu edit=new Menu("Edit");
MenuItem item5,item6,item7,item8;
edit.add(item5=new MenuItem("Cut"));
edit.add(item6=new MenuItem("Copy"));
edit.add(item7=new MenuItem("Paste"));
edit.add(item8=new MenuItem("SelectAll"));
mbar.add(edit);                   //Adding Menu to Menu
Bar//
item5.addActionListener(this);
item6.addActionListener(this);
item7.addActionListener(this);
item8.addActionListener(this);
addWindowListener(new WindowAdapter(){
public void windowClosing(WindowEvent me)
{
      setVisible(false);
}
});
}

public void actionPerformed(ActionEvent ae)
{
 str=ae.getActionCommand();
if(str.equals("Open"))
{
   new MenuFiguresDemo().open();
}
}
public void paint(Graphics g)
{
```

(Contd.)

```
 }
 }
public class MenuFiguresDemo
{
 Frame f;
MenuFiguresDemo ()
{
f=new MenuFrameDemo("Making a simple application");
f.setVisible(true);
}
public static void main(String s[])
 {
new  MenuFiguresDemo();

 }

public void open()
{
 FileDialog fd=new FileDialog(f,"file dialog");
   fd.setVisible(true);
}
}
```

Program 49.

```
// program to make a moving ball

import java.awt.*;
import java.awt.event.*;
import java.applet.*;
public class Moving_Ball extends Applet implements
KeyListener
{
 int x1=200,y1=200,code;
 public void init()
  {
   setBackground(Color.blue);
   addKeyListener(this);
   requestFocus();
  }
 public void keyPressed(KeyEvent ke)
  {
    code=ke.getKeyCode();
```

(Contd.)

```
    if(x1==560)
      x1=0;
    if(y1==360)
      y1=0;
    if(x1<0)
      x1=560;
    if(y1<0)
      y1=360;
    switch(code)
     {
       case KeyEvent.VK_LEFT:
          x1--;
          break;
       case KeyEvent.VK_RIGHT:
          x1++;
          break;
       case KeyEvent.VK_UP:
          y1--;
          break;
       case KeyEvent.VK_DOWN:
          y1++;
          break;
     }
    repaint();
  }
public void keyReleased(KeyEvent ke){}
public void keyTyped(KeyEvent ke){}
public void paint(Graphics g)
 {
  g.setColor(Color.orange);
  g.drawOval(x1,y1,40,40);
  g.setColor(Color.red);
  g.fillOval(x1+1,y1+1,39,39);
 }
}
```

Program 50.

```
// program to move a banner through the screen

import java.awt.*;
import java.applet.*;
public class MovingBanner extends Applet implements
```

(Contd.)

```
Runnable
{
 Thread t;
 int x,y;
 String msg="Hello Java";
 public void init()
  {
   setBackground(Color.black);
   setForeground(Color.orange);
    t=new Thread(this);
    x=10;
    y=10;
  }
 public void start()
  {
   t.start();
  }
 public void run()
 {
  char ch;
  int flag=0;
  while(true)
   {
    repaint();
    try
     {
     Thread.sleep(200);
     }
    catch(Exception e)
     {
      }
    if(flag==0 && x<600)
      {
        x=x+10;
      }
    else
     {
      if(x>=0)
     {
      x=x-10;
      flag=1;
     }
    else
```

(Contd.)

```
      flag=0;
    }
  }
 }
 public void paint(Graphics g)
  {
  g.drawString(msg,x,y);
  }
}
```

Program 51.

```
// program to make multiple threads

class MultiThread implements Runnable
{
 Thread t;
 MultiThread(String s)
  {
   t=new Thread(this,s);
   t.start();
  }
 public void run()
  {
    try
     {
     for(int i=0;i<5;i++)
      {
        System.out.println(t+" "+i);
        Thread.sleep(200);
      }
     }
    catch(InterruptedException e)
      {
      System.out.println(e);
      }
   System.out.println("Exiting child Thread:"+t);
  }
}
class MulThreadDemo
 {
   public static void main(String args[])
```

(Contd.)

```
    {
     MultiThread ml1=new MultiThread("one");
     MultiThread ml2=new MultiThread("two");
     MultiThread ml3=new MultiThread("three");
      try
       {
        for(int i=0;i<5;i++)
         {
           System.out.println("Main Thread "+i);
          Thread.sleep(1000);
             }
       }
      catch(InterruptedException e)
       {
        System.out.println(e);
       }
     System.out.println("Exiting main Thread");
    }
 }
```

Program 52.

```
// program to make a multiple threads and using
join method

class MultiThread implements Runnable
{
 Thread t;
 MultiThread(String s)
  {
    t=new Thread(this,s);
    t.start();
  }
 public void run()
  {
    try
     {
     for(int i=0;i<5;i++)
       {
        System.out.println(t+" "+i);
        Thread.sleep(200);
       }
     }
```

(Contd.)

```
      catch(Exception e)
       {
       System.out.println(e);
       }
    System.out.println("Exiting child Thread:"+t);
  }
}
class MulThreadDemo1
 {
   public static void main(String args[])
     {
       try
        {

      MultiThread ml1=new MultiThread("one");

       ml1.t.join();
      System.out.println(ml1.t.isAlive());
      MultiThread ml2=new MultiThread("two");
       ml2.t.join();
      MultiThread ml3=new MultiThread("three");
       ml3.t.join();
         }
        catch(Exception e)
         {
           System.out.println(e);
         }
       System.out.println("Exiting main Thread");
     }
  }
```

Program 53.

```
 // a simple program of nested try catch blocks

 class Multi
 {
  public static void main(String args[])
   {
     try
      {
        int a=args.length;
        int b=50;
```

(Contd.)

```
        System.out.println("a="+a);
          try
           {
             if(a==1)
               a=a/(a-a);
            System.out.println("First");
             if(a==2)
               {
                 int c[]={1};
                 c[20]=56;
            System.out.println("Second");
               }
            }
     catch(ArrayIndexOutOfBoundsException e)
      {
      System.out.println(e);
      System.out.println("Third");
      }
   }
        catch(ArithmeticException e)
      {
      System.out.println(e);
      }
   }
}
```

Program 54.

```
// program to show multiple ca' 'hes with a single
try

class MultipleCatch
{
 public static void main(String args[])
  {
    int x=args.length;
    int y=10;
    try
     {
       int z=y/x;
```

(Contd.)

```
        System.out.println(z);
        int arr[]={1,2,3,4};
        arr[30]=10;
       System.out.println("array testing");
      }
     catch(ArithmeticException e)
       {
        System.out.println(e);
       }
     catch(ArrayIndexOutOfBoundsException e)
       {
        System.out.println(e);
       }
   }
}
```

Program 55.

```
// program to draw figures at the press of the key

import java.applet.*;
import java.awt.*;
import java.awt.event.*;
public class MultipleDraw extends Applet implements
KeyListener
{
 public void init()
  {
  addKeyListener(this);
   requestFocus();
  setBackground(Color.pink);
  }
 public void keyPressed(KeyEvent ke)
  {
  int i=ke.getKeyCode();
  Graphics g=getGraphics();
  switch(i)
    {
     case KeyEvent.VK_R:
                  g.drawRect(10,20,50,60);
                  break;
     case KeyEvent.VK_L :
```

(Contd.)

```
                    g.drawLine(100,120,100,500);
                     break;
        case KeyEvent.VK_C:
                    g.drawOval(50,70,100,120);
                    g.setColor(Color.yellow);
                    g.fillOval(51,71,99,119);
                     break;
      }

      }

   public void keyReleased(KeyEvent ke){}
   public void keyTyped(KeyEvent ke){}
   public void paint(Graphics g)
  {
  }

  }
```

Program 56.

```
// program to show the concept of inner classes

import java.applet.*;
import java.awt.*;
import java.awt.event.*;
import java.util.*;
public class MyApplet extends Applet
 {
  public void init()
    {
    addMouseListener(new MyMouseAdapter(this));
    }
 }
 class MyMouseAdapter extends MouseAdapter
 {
  MyApplet myapp;
  MyMouseAdapter(MyApplet temp)
    {
     myapp=temp;
    }
  public void mousePressed(MouseEvent me)
    {
```

(Contd.)

```
    myapp.showStatus("Mouse Pressed");
    }
  }
```

Program 57.

```
// client program for the chat application

import java.io.*;
import java.net.*;
class new_cha client1
{
    public static void main(String args[])
    {
        try{
        Socket s=new Socket("192.168.0.45",8189);
        ObjectInputStream from_server=new
ObjectInputStream(s.getInputStream());
        BufferedReader from_console=new
BufferedReader(new InputStreamReader(System.in));
        ObjectOutputStream to_server=new
ObjectOutputStream(s.getOutputStream());
        String str_from_server,str_from_console;

System.out.println(from_server.readObject());
        while(true)
        {

str_from_server=(String)from_server.readObject();//
waiting for server to give response
            if(str_from_server==null ||
str_from_server.equalsIgnoreCase("bye"))
                break;
            System.out.println("Message Recieved-->
"+str_from_server);
            System.out.print("Write Message--->");
            str_from_console=from_console.readLine();
            to_server.writeObject(str_from_console);
            to_server.flush();
            if(str_from_console==null ||
str_from_console.equalsIgnoreCase("bye"))
                break;
```

(Contd.)

```
        }
        from_server.close();
        to_server.close();
        from_console.close();
        }
        catch(Exception e){System.out.println(e);}
    }
}
```

Program 58.

```
// server program for the chat application

import  java.io.*;
import java.net.*;
public class new_chatserver1
{
    public static void main(String args[])
    {
        try{
        ServerSocket ss=new ServerSocket(8189);
        System.out.println("Server Started");
        System.out.println("Server Inet Address :
"+InetAddress.getLocalHost());
        System.out.println("Port No : 8189");
        Socket client1=null;
        Socket client2 =null;
        int count=0;

        while(true)
        {
            if(count==2)
            {
                count=0;
                new new_server1(client1,client2);
            }
            client1=ss.accept();
            count++;
            client2=ss.accept();
            count++;
        }
        }
        catch(Exception e){}
```

(Contd.)

```
    }
}

class new_server1 implements Runnable,Serializable
{
    Thread t;
    Socket client1,client2;
    new_server1(Socket s1,Socket s2)
    {
        client1=s1;
        client2=s2;
        t=new Thread(this);
        t.start();
    }
    public void run()
    {
        try{
        String str1="Welcome to Chatting";
        String str2="Welcome to Chatting";
        int flag1=0,flag2=0;
        ObjectOutputStream to_client1=new
ObjectOutputStream(client1.getOutputStream());
        ObjectOutputStream to_client2=new
ObjectOutputStream(client2.getOutputStream());
        ObjectInputStream from_client1=new
ObjectInputStream(client1.getInputStream());
        ObjectInputStream from_client2=new
ObjectInputStream(client2.getInputStream());
        to_client1.writeObject("You have been
Connected to : "+client2.getInetAddress());
        to_client2.writeObject("You have been
Connected to : "+client1.getInetAddress());
        while(true)
        {
            to_client1.writeObject(str2);
            to_client1.flush();
            if(str2==null   ||
str2.equalsIgnoreCase("bye"))
                flag1=1;
            if(flag1==1 && flag2==1)
                t.stop();
            str1=(String)from_client1.readObject();
            to_client2.writeObject(str1);
```

(Contd.)

```
            to_client2.flush();
            if(str1==null ||
str1 .equalsIgnoreCase("bye") )
                flag2=1;
            if(flag1==1 && flag2==1)
                t.stop();

            str2=(String)from_client2.readObject();

        }
        }
        catch(Exception e){System.out.println(e);}
    }
}
```

Program 59.

```
// Overriding functions

class A
{
public void display()
{
System.out.println("DISPLAY FUNCTION OF CLASS A
CALLED");
}
}

class OverRidden extends A
{
public void display()
{
//super.display();             DISPLAYED ABOVE
System.out.println("DISPLAY FUNCTION OF MAIN
CALLED");
super.display();              //DISPLAYED BELOW
}
public static void main(String args[])
{
OverRidden b=new OverRidden();
b.display();
}
}
```

Program 60.

```
// Producer Consumer problem

class Q
{
 int n;
 boolean flag=false;
 synchronized int get()
  {
   if(flag)
    {
     try
      {
       wait();
      }
    catch(InterruptedException e)
      {
      System.out.println(e);
      }
     }
    System.out.println("got:"+n);
     flag=false;
     notify();
     return n;
  }
 synchronized int put(int n)
  {
   if(!flag)
    {
     try
      {
       wait();
      }
    catch(InterruptedException e)
      {
      System.out.println(e);
      }
    }
     this.n=n;
     flag=true;
    System.out.println("put:"+n);
```

(Contd.)

```
    notify();
    return n;
  }

}//end of class q

class Producer implements Runnable
{
 Q q;
 Thread t;
 Producer(Q q)
 {
  this.q=q;
  t=new Thread(this,"producer");
  t.start();
 }
 public void run()
  {
   int i=0;
   while(i<=10)
    {
     q.put(i++);
    }
  }
}
class Consumer implements Runnable
{
 Q q;
 Thread t;
 Consumer(Q q)
 {
  this.q=q;
  t=new Thread(this,"consumer");
  t.start();
 }
 public void run()
  {
    while(true)
    {
    q.get();
    }
  }
}
```

(Contd.)

```
class PCFixed
{
 public static void main(String args[])
  {
   Q q=new Q();
   Producer p=new Producer(q);
   Consumer c=new Consumer(q);
   try
    {
     p.t.join();
     c.t.join();
    }
   catch(Exception e)
    {
    System.out.println(e);
    }
  }
}
```

Program 61.

```
// program to make radio buttons

import java.applet.*;
import java.awt.*;
import java.awt.event.*;
public class RadioButtonDemo extends Applet
implements ItemListener
{
 String str="";
 CheckboxGroup cbg;
 Checkbox cb1,cb2,cb3,cb4;
 public void init()
  {
   cbg=new CheckboxGroup();
   cb1=new Checkbox("Delhi",cbg,true);
   cb2=new Checkbox("Mumbai",cbg,false);
   cb3=new Checkbox("Chennai",cbg,false);
   cb4=new Checkbox("Calcutta",cbg,false);
    add(cb1);
    add(cb2);
    add(cb3);
```

(Contd.)

```
    add(cb4);
    cb1.addItemListener(this);
    cb2.addItemListener(this);
    cb3.addItemListener(this);
    cb4.addItemListener(this);
    }
  public void itemStateChanged(ItemEvent ie)
    {
         repaint();
    }
  public void paint(Graphics g)
    {
   g.drawString(cbg.getSelectedCheckbox().getLabel()
 +  " selected",10,60);
    }
 }
```

Program 62.

```
// program to draw a rectangle by dragging

import java.awt.*;
import java.awt.event.*;
import java.applet.*;
public class RectDrag extends Applet implements
MouseListener,MouseMotionListener
{
 int x1,y1,x2,y2;
 Graphics g;
 public void init()
  {
   addMouseListener(this);
   addMouseMotionListener(this);
   requestFocus();
   g=getGraphics();
  }
 public void mousePressed(MouseEvent me)
   {
  x1=me.getX();
  y1=me.getY();
   }
 public void mouseClicked(MouseEvent me){}
```

(Contd.)

```
public void mouseReleased(MouseEvent me)
{
 x2=me.getX();
 y2=me.getY();

 repaint();
}
public void mouseEntered(MouseEvent me){}
public void mouseExited(MouseEvent me){}
public void mouseMoved(MouseEvent me){}
public void mouseDragged(MouseEvent me)
  {}
public void paint(Graphics g)
 {
  g.setColor(Color.blue);
  g.drawRect(x1,y1,x2,y2);
  g.setColor(Color.red);
  g.fillRect(x1+1,y1+1,x2-1,y2-1);
  }
}
```

Program 63.

```
class NewThread implements Runnable
{
 Thread t;
 String name;
 NewThread(String n)
 {
  name=n;
  t=new Thread(this,name);
  t.start();
 }
 public void run()
 {
  try
   {
    for(int i=10;i>=0;i--)
       {
       System.out.println(t+" "+i);
       Thread.sleep(250);
       }
```

(Contd.)

```
    }
   catch(InterruptedException e)
    {
     System.out.println(e);
    }
  }
}

class Resume
{
 public static void main(String args[])
  {
   NewThread ob1=new NewThread("one");
   NewThread ob2=new NewThread("two");
    try
    {
     Thread.sleep(1000);
     ob1.t.suspend();
     System.out.println("Suspending Thread one");
     Thread.sleep(1000);
     ob1.t.resume();
     System.out.println("Resuming Thread one");
     Thread.sleep(1000);
     ob2.t.suspend();
     System.out.println("Suspending Thread two");
     Thread.sleep(1000);
     ob2.t.resume();
     System.out.println("Resuming Thread two");
     ob1.t.join();
     ob2.t.join();
    }
   catch(InterruptedException e)
     {
      System.out.println(e);
     }
   }
}
```

Program 64.

```
// program to sort numbers using selection sort

class SelStrSort
{
```

(Contd.)

```
    public static void main(String s[])
     {
      String temp;
       for(int i=0;i<s.length;i++)
          {
            for(int j=i+1;j<s.length;j++)
               {
               if((s[i].compareTo(s[j]))>0)
                 {
                    temp=s[i];
                    s[i]=s[j];
                    s[j]=temp;

                  }

                }
             }
       for(int i=0;i<s.length;i++)
          System.out.println(s[i]);
       }
 }
```

Program 65.

```
// program to depict serialization

class SerailizeMe implements Serializable
 {
  int i;
  float f;
  String s;
  SerializeMe(int x,float y,String str)
   {
    i=x;
    f=y;
    s=str;
   }
 }
class SerializationDemo
 {
  public static void main(String args[])
   {
```

(Contd.)

```
    try
    {
    SerializeMe obj=new SerializeMe
(2,14.76,"hello");
    FileOutputAStream fos=new
FileOutputStream("mca.txt");
    ObjectOutStream oos=new
ObjectOutputStream(fos);
    oos.writeObject(obj);
    oos.flush();
    fos.close();
    }
   catch(Exception e)
    {
    System.out.println(e);
    }
    try
     {
     SerializeMe ob1;
     FileInputStream fis=new
FileInputStream("mca.txt");
     ObjectInputStream ois=new
ObjectInputStream(fis);
    ob1=(SerializeMe)ois.readObject();
     ob1.display();
     ois.close();
     }
    catch(Exception e)
    {
    System.out.println(e);
    }
  }
}
```

Program 66.

```
// program for server

import java.io.*;
import java.net.*;
class ServerProgram
{
    public static void main(String args[])
```

(Contd.)

```
    {

    try
    {

System.out.println(InetAddress.getLocalHost());
        ServerSocket ss=new ServerSocket(8189);
        Socket s=ss.accept();
        System.out.println("Server is connected with
: "+s.getInetAddress());
        ObjectInputStream ois=new
ObjectInputStream(s.getInputStream());

        while(true)
        {
            String str=(String)ois.readObject();

            if(str.equalsIgnoreCase("bye"))
                break;
            System.out.println(str);
        }
    }
    catch(Exception e)
    {
        System.out.println(e);
    }

    }
}
```

Program 67.

```
// program for the JDBC connectivity through
servlets

import java.io.*;
import javax.servlet.*;
import javax.servlet.http.*;
public class SessionTracker extends HttpServlet
{
 public void doGet(HttpServletRequest
req,HttpServletResponse res)throws
IOException,ServletException
```

(Contd.)

```
  {
    doPost(req,res);
  }
 public void doPost(HttpServletRequest
req,HttpServletResponse res)throws
IOException,ServletException
  {
  res.setContentType("Text/html");
  PrintWriter out=res.getWriter();


   // get the current session object if necessary
  HttpSession session=req.getSession(true);
   // increment the hit counter for this page
  // the value is saved in this client's session
under the name HITS
 Integer count=(Integer)session.getValue("HITS");

 if(count!=null)
  {
  count=new Integer(count.intValue()+1);
  }
 else
  count=new Integer(1);
 session.putValue("HITS",count);
 out.println("<HTML><BODY>");
 out.println("<h1>You have visited this
page"+count+"times</h1>");
 out.println("</body></html>");
 }
}
```

Program 68.

```
// program to make a single try catch block

class SingleCatch
{
 public static void main(String args[])
  {
   int i=10;
   int j=0;
```

(Contd.)

```
    int k;
    for(j=-5;j<=5;j++)
     {
       try
        {
         k=i/j;
         System.out.println(k);
        }
      catch(ArithmeticException e)
        {
         System.out.println("Divide by zero
error");
         System.out.println(e);
        }
      }
      System.out.println("Exiting main");
    }
}
```

Program 69.

```
// program to sort numbers using bubble sort

class Sort
{
  public static void main(String s[])
   {
    String temp;
     for(int i=0;i<s.length;i++)
        {
         for(int j=0;j<s.length-1;j++)
            {
        if(Integer.parseInt(s[j])>Integer.parseInt(s[j+1]))
               {
                temp=s[j];
                s[j]=s[j+1];
                s[j+1]=temp;

               }

            }
         }
```

(Contd.)

```
      for(int i=0;i<s.length;i++)
         System.out.println(s[i]);
      }
   }
```

Program 70.

```
// program to implement stack

import javax.swing.*;
class Stack
{
private int arr[];
private int top;
public Stack(int x)
{
 top=-1;
 arr=new int[x];
}
public void push(int x)
{
 top++;
 if(top>arr.length-1)
  {
   System.out.println("Stack is full");
   System.exit(1);
  }
  else
   arr[top]=x;
}
public int pop()
{
  int x=0;
  if(top==-1)
   {
   System.out.println("Stack is empty");
   System.exit(1);
   }
  else
    x=arr[top-1];
    top--;
    return x;
```

(Contd.)

```
}
}
class StackDemo
{
   public static void main(String args[])
     {
        int n;
      n=Integer.parseInt(JOptionPane.showInputDialog("Enter
the stack length:"));
        Stack s1=new Stack(n);
        try
        {
        for(int i=0;i<=n;i++)
          s1.push(i);
        for(int i=0;i<=n;i++)
         System.out.println(s1.pop());
        }
        catch(Exception e)
         {
         System.out.println(e);
         }
     }
}
```

Program 71.

```
// program to show inheritance

import javax.swing.*;
class Staff
{
 int code;
 String name;
 Staff(){}
 Staff(int c,String s)
  {
   code=c;
   name=s;
  }
 public void get()
  {
   code=Integer.parseInt(JOptionPane.showInputDialog("Enter
the code"));
```

(Contd.)

```
    name=JOptionPane.showInputDialog("Enter the
     name");
   }
  public void display()
   {
    JOptionPane.showMessageDialog(null,"code:
     "+code);
    JOptionPane.showMessageDialog(null,"name:
     "+name);
   }
  public static void main(String args[])
   {
     Staff s;
     s=new Teacher();
     s.get();
     s.display();
     s=new Officer();
     s.get();
     s.display();
     s=new Regular();
     s.get();
     s.display();
     s=new Casual();
     s.get();
     s.display();

   }
}
class Teacher extends Staff
{
  String subject;
  Teacher(){}
  Teacher(int c,String s,String s1)
   {
     super(c,s);
     subject=s1;
   }

  public void get()
   {
    super.get();
   subject=JOptionPane.showInputDialog("Enter the
```

(Contd.)

```
subject");
   }
  public void display()
   {
    super.display();
    JOptionPane.showMessageDialog(null,"subject:
    "+subject);
   }
}
class Officer extends Staff
{
   String grade;
   Officer(){}
   Officer(int c,String s,String g)
    {
      super(c,s);
      grade=g;
    }

  public void get()
    {
     super.get();
     grade=JOptionPane.showInputDialog("Enter the
     grade");
    }
  public void display()
    {
     super.display();
     JOptionPane.showMessageDialog(null,"grade:
     "+grade);
    }
}
class Typist extends Staff
{
   int speed;
   Typist(){}
   Typist(int c,String s,int s2)
    {
      super(c,s);
      speed=s2;
    }
```

(Contd.)

```
public void get()
 {
  super.get();
  speed=Integer.parseInt(JOptionPane.showInputDialog
  ("Enter the speed of the typist"));
 }
public void display()
 {
  super.display();
  JOptionPane.showMessageDialog(null,"speed:
  "+speed);
 }
}
class Regular extends Typist
{
 Regular(){}
 Regular(int c,String s,int s2)
  {
   super(c,s,s2);
  }

 public void get()
  {
   super.get();
  }
 public void display()
  {
   super.display();
  }
}
class Casual extends Typist
{
 int wages;
  Casual(){}
  Casual(int c,String s,int s2,int w)
  {
   super(c,s,s2);
   wages=w;
  }

 public void get()
  {
   super.get();
```

(Contd.)

```
   wages=Integer.parseInt(JOptionPane.showInputDialog("Enter
the wages"));
   }
  public void display()
   {
    super.display();
   JOptionPane.showMessageDialog(null,"wages:
"+wages);
   }
}
```

Program 72.

```
// program to show the working of static variables

class StaticDemo
{
  static int count;
  static
  {
    count=0;
   System.out.println("static block called");
  }
  StaticDemo()
   {
    count++;
   }
  public static void main(String args[])
   {
     StaticDemo s1=new StaticDemo();
     StaticDemo s2=new StaticDemo();
     System.out.println("number of objects
created"+count);
     StaticDemo1 s11=new StaticDemo1();
     StaticDemo1 s21=new StaticDemo1();
     System.out.println("number of objects
created"+StaticDemo1.getcount());
      }
}

class StaticDemo1
{
  static int count1;
```

(Contd.)

```
  static
  {
    count1=0;
   System.out.println("static block of staticdemo1
called");
  }
  StaticDemo1()
   {
    count1++;
   }
  static int getcount()
   {
     return count1;
   }
 }
```

Program 73.

```
// program which takes the stream based input
output

import java.io.*;
class Streams1
{
 public static void main(String args[])
  {
    FileOutputStream fos=null;
    FileInputStream fis=null;
     int i=0;
    String str[]=new String[100];
    System.out.println("Enter few lines of
text.Type stop when you finish");
     try
      {
      BufferedReader br=new BufferedReader(new
InputStreamReader(System.in));
     while(!((str[i]=br.readLine()).equals("stop")))
        i++;
       fos=new FileOutputStream("stream1.txt");
        for(int j=0;j<i;j++)
          {
           for(int k=0;k<str[j].length();k++)
```

(Contd.)

```
          {
           fos.write(str[j].charAt(k));
          }
        fos.write('\n');
       }
      fos.close();
     }
    catch(Exception e)
     {
      System.out.println(e);
     }
     try
     {
       int b;
      fis=new FileInputStream("stream1.txt");
      while((b=fis.read())!=-1)
        {
         if((char)b=='\n')
           System.out.println();
         else
            System.out.println((char)b);
        }
       fis.close();
      }
     catch(Exception e1)
        {
        System.out.println(e1);
        }
     }
}
```

Program 84.

```
// program to show suspending & resuming of threads

class NewThread implements Runnable
{
 call1 c;
 Thread t;
 String name;
 NewThread(String n)
  {
```

(Contd.)

```
   name=n;
   t=new Thread(this,name);
   t.start();
  }
 public void run()
  {
   int i=0;
   while(i<=20)
   {
    c.first();
    i++;
   }
  }
}
class call1
{
 boolean flag=false;
 synchronized void first()
  {
   if(!flag)
    {
     try
      {
       for(int i=20;i>=0;i--)
        {
        System.out.println(t+" "+i);
         wait();
        }
      }
    catch(InterruptedException e)
      {
       System.out.println(e);
      }
    }
  }
}

class SuspendResume
{
 public static void main(String args[])
  {
   call1 c=new call1();
   NewThread ob1=new NewThread("one");
```

(Contd.)

```
 NewThread ob2=new NewThread("two");
  try
  {
  Thread.sleep(1000);

  System.out.println("Suspending Thread one");
  Thread.sleep(1000);
  ob1.t.resume();
  System.out.println("Resuming Thread one");
  ob2.t.suspend();
  System.out.println("Suspending Thread two");
  ob2.t.resume();
  System.out.println("Resuming Thread two");
  ob1.t.join();
  ob2.t.join();
  }
 catch(InterruptedException e)
   {
   System.out.println(e);
   }
 }
}
```

Program 75.

```
class call1
 {
  boolean flag=false;
  synchronized void mysuspend()
   {
    flag=false;
    wait();
   }
  synchronized void myresume()
   {
    flag=true;
    notify();
   }
 }
class NewThread implements Runnable
{
 call1 c;
 Thread t;
```

(Contd.)

```
NewThread(call1 temp,String s)
 {
  c=temp;
  t=new Thread(this,"one");
  c.flag=false;
  t.start();
 }
 public void run()
 {
  try
  {
   for(int i=10;i>=0;i--)
    {
     System.out.println(t+" "+i);
     Thread.sleep(200);
    }
   }
   catch(InterruptedException e)
    {
    System.out.println(e);
    }
  }
}
class SuspendResume1
{
 call1 c=new call1();
 NewThread ob1=new NewThread(c,"one");
 NewThread ob2=new NewThread(c,"two");
 Thread.sleep(1000);
 ob1.t.mysuspend();
 System.out.println("Suspending thread one");
 Thread.sleep(1000);
 ob1.t.myresume();
 System.out.println("Resuming thread one");
 ob2.t.mysuspend();
 System.out.println("Suspending thread two");
 Thread.sleep(1000);
 ob2.t.myresume();
 System.out.println("Resuming thread two");
 ob1.t.join();
 ob2.t.join();
 }
catch(InterruptedException e)
```

(Contd.)

```
{
 System.out.println(e);
}
}
```

Program 76.

```
// program for printing the desired output

class callme
{
  void call(String s)
   {
   System.out.print("["+s);
try
{
Thread.sleep(500);
}
catch(InterruptedException e)
{
   System.out.print(e);
}
   System.out.println("]");
}
}
class caller implements Runnable
{
String msg;
Thread t;
callme c;
caller(callme temp,String s)
{
msg=s;
c=temp;
t=new Thread(this);
t.start();
}
public void run()
{
c.call(msg);
}
}
```

(Contd.)

```
class syncdemo
{
public static void main(String args[])
{
callme c=new callme();
caller obj1=new caller(c,"hello");
caller obj2=new caller(c,"synchronized");
caller obj3=new caller(c,"world");
try
{
obj1.t.join();
obj2.t.join();
obj3.t.join();
}
catch(InterruptedException e)
{
   System.out.print(e);
}
}
}
```

Program 77.

```
class call1 extends callme
{
 synchronized void xyz(String s)
  {
    call(s);
  }
}
class caller implements Runnable
{
String msg;
Thread t;
call1 c;
caller(call1 temp,String s)
{
msg=s;
c=temp;
t=new Thread(this);
t.start();
```

(Contd.)

```
}
public void run()
{
c.xyz(msg);
}
}
class syncdemo1
{
public static void main(String args[])
{
call1 c=new call1();
caller obj1=new caller(c,"hello");
caller obj2=new caller(c,"synchronized");
caller obj3=new caller(c,"world");
try
{
obj1.t.join();
obj2.t.join();
obj3.t.join();
}
catch(InterruptedException e)
{
   System.out.print(e);
}
}
}
```

Program 78.

```
// program to make a textbox

import java.applet.*;
import java.awt.*;
import java.awt.event.*;
public class TextBoxDemo extends Applet implements
ActionListener
{
 TextField t1,t2;
  public void init()
  {
  t1=new TextField(15);
  t2=new TextField(15);
```

(Contd.)

```
  add(t1);
  add(t2);
  t1.addActionListener(this);
  t2.addActionListener(this);
 }
 public void actionPerformed(ActionEvent ae)
  {
    repaint();
  }
 public void paint(Graphics g)
  {
   g.drawString(t1.getSelectedText(),10,50);
   g.drawString(t2.getText(),10,80);
  }
}
```

Program 79.

```
// program to create child thread from main thread

class NewThread implements Runnable
{
  Thread t;
  NewThread()
   {
    t=new Thread(this,"Child thread");
    System.out.println("Child thread"+t);
    t.start();
   }
  public void run()
   {
     try
      {
          for(int i=0;i<5;i++)
           {
           System.out.println("Child thread"+i);
            Thread.sleep(500);
           }
      }
     catch(InterruptedException e)
       {
         System.out.println(e);
```

(Contd.)

```
        }
      System.out.println("Child thread exiting");
      }
}
class ThreadDem
{
  public static void main(String args[])
   {
     NewThread n1=new NewThread();
      try
       {
         for(int i=0;i<5;i++)
          {
           System.out.println("Main thread"+i);
           Thread.sleep(1000);
          }
       }
      catch(InterruptedException e)
        {
         System.out.println(e);
        }
      System.out.println("main thread exiting");
    }
}
}
```

Program 80.

```
// program to name a thread

class ThreadDemo
 {
   public static void main(String args[])
    {
     Thread t=Thread.currentThread();
     System.out.println("Current thread"+t);
     t.setName("My Thread");
     System.out.println("After name change"+t);
      try
       {
         for(int i=0;i<=5;i++)
          {
```

(Contd.)

```
            System.out.println(i);
            Thread.sleep(1000);
          }
       }
      catch(InterruptedException e)
        {
         System.out.println(e);
        }
     }
  }
```

Program 81.

```
// program to terminate all the child threads
before main thread terminates

class NewThread implements Runnable
{
  Thread t;
  NewThread()
   {
    t=new Thread(this,"Child thread");
    System.out.println("Child thread"+t);
    t.start();
   }
  public void run()
   {
     try
      {
         for(int i=0;i<5;i++)
          {
          System.out.println("Child thread"+i);
            Thread.sleep(500);
          }
      }
     catch(InterruptedException e)
       {
        System.out.println(e);
       }
    System.out.println("Child thread exiting");
    }
}
```

(Contd.)

```
class ThreadDemo1
{
  public static void main(String args[])
   {
      NewThread n1=new NewThread();
       try
        {
          for(int i=0;i<5;i++)
            {
             System.out.println("Main thread"+i);
              Thread.sleep(1000);
            }
         }
        catch(InterruptedException e)
          {
           System.out.println(e);
          }
        System.out.println("main thread exiting");
    }
}
}
```

Program 82.

```
// program to add two times

 class Time
{
int hour;
int min;
int sec;

Time()
{
hour=-1;
min=-1;
sec=-1;
}
Time(int h,int m,int s)
{
hour=h;
min=m;
```

(Contd.)

```
sec=s;
}

Time add(Time t)
{
Time temp=new Time();
temp.hour=hour+t.hour;
temp.min=min+t.min;
temp.sec=sec+t.sec;

while(temp.sec >= 60)
{
    temp.min+=1;
    temp.sec-=60;
}

while(temp.min >=60)
{
    temp.hour+=1;
    temp.min-=60;
}
return temp;
}

void display()
{
System.out.println(hour+" "+min+" "+sec);
}

public static void main(String args[])
{

Time t1=new Time(10,3,61);
Time t2=new Time(10,13,12);
Time t3=t1.add(t2);
t3.display();
}
}
```

(Contd.)

Program 83.

```
// program to show inheritance

class Vehicle
{
 int wheelcount;
 String name;
 Vehicle()
 {}
 Vehicle(int w,String n)
  {
   wheelcount=w;
   name=n;
  }
 public void display()
  {
   System.out.println("The no of wheels
is:"+wheelcount);
   System.out.println("The name of the vehicle
is:"+name);
  }
 //main function
 public static void main(String args[])
  {
   Vehicle v;
   v=new GearedMotor(4,"car",120,4);
   v.display();
   v=new NonGearedMotor(2,"bicycle",5);
   v.display();
   v=new Passenger(6,"bus","uptill 2005",60,30,20);
   v.display();
   v=new Goods(6,"truck","uptill 2003",100);
   v.display();
  }
}
class LightMotor extends Vehicle
{
 int speedcount;
 LightMotor()
 {}
 LightMotor(int w,String n,int s)
```

(Contd.)

```
  {
   super(w,n);
   speedcount=s;
  }
 public void display()
   {
    super.display();
    System.out.println("The speed of the vehicle
is:"+speedcount);
   }
}

class HeavyMotor extends Vehicle
{
 String permit;
 int loadcapacity;
 HeavyMotor()
  {}
 HeavyMotor(int w,String n,String p,int l)
  {
   super(w,n);
   permit=p;
   loadcapacity=l;
  }
 public void display()
   {
    super.display();
    System.out.println("The permit no of the vehicle
is:"+permit);
    System.out.println("The load capacity of the
vehicle is:"+loadcapacity);
   }
}
class GearedMotor extends LightMotor
{
 int gearcount;
 GearedMotor()
  {}
 GearedMotor(int w,String n,int s,int g)
  {
   super(w,n,s);
```

(Contd.)

```
  gearcount=g;
 }
 public void display()
  {
   super.display();
   System.out.println("The  no of gears the vehicle
has:"+gearcount);
  }
}
class NonGearedMotor extends LightMotor
{

 NonGearedMotor()
 {}
 NonGearedMotor(int w,String n,int s)
 {
  super(w,n,s);
   }
 public void display()
  {
   super.display();
  }
}

class Passenger extends HeavyMotor
{
 int sitting;
 int standing;
 Passenger()
 {}
 Passenger(int w,String n,String p,int l,int s1,int
s2)
 {
  super(w,n,p,l);
  sitting=s1;
  standing=s2;
 }
 public void display()
  {
   super.display();
   System.out.println("The  no of persons sitting
in the vehicle is:"+sitting);
   System.out.println("The no of persons standing
```

(Contd.)

```
in the vehicle is:"+standing);
  }
}
class Goods extends HeavyMotor
{
 Goods()
 {}
 Goods(int w,String n,String p,int l)
 {
  super(w,n,p,l);
 }
 public void display()
  {
  super.display();
  }
}
```

Index

□□□